THE SUBSTANCE OF REPRESENTATION

PRINCETON STUDIES IN AMERICAN POLITICS
HISTORICAL, INTERNATIONAL, AND COMPARATIVE PERSPECTIVES

SERIES EDITORS
Ira Katznelson, Martin Shefter, Theda Skocpol

A list of titles
in this series appears
at the back of
the book

THE SUBSTANCE
OF REPRESENTATION

CONGRESS, AMERICAN POLITICAL
DEVELOPMENT, AND LAWMAKING

John S. Lapinski

PRINCETON UNIVERSITY PRESS
PRINCETON AND OXFORD

Requests for permission to reproduce material from this work should be
sent to permissions, Princeton University Press.
Published by Princeton University Press, 41 William Street,
Princeton, New Jersey 08540
In the United Kingdom: Princeton University Press,
6 Oxford Street, Woodstock, Oxfordshire OX20 1TW

press.princeton.edu

Library of Congress Cataloging-in-Publication Data

Lapinski, John S., 1967–
The substance of representation : Congress, American political development, and
lawmaking / John S. Lapinski.
pages cm
Includes bibliographical references and index.
ISBN 978-0-691-13781-0 (hardcover : alk. paper) – ISBN 978-0-691-13782-7
(pbk. : alk. paper)
1. United States. Congress.   2. Legislation–United States.
3. United States–Politics and government.   I. Title.
JK1021.L37 2013
328.73–dc23
2013013888

British Library Cataloging-in-Publication Data is available

This book has been composed in Minion Pro

Printed on acid-free paper ∞

Typeset by S R Nova Pvt Ltd, Bangalore, India
Printed in the United States of America

10 9 8 7 6 5 4 3 2 1

Contents

Preface

IN WRITING THIS BOOK, I often thought about Sisyphus. In Greek mythology, he was the king who was punished by being forced to roll an immense boulder up a hill only to watch it roll back down. My metaphorical boulder involved collecting more data and creating better measures of lawmaking. Fortunately, I was not compelled to repeat this action forever (though it felt like it). Of course, I didn't make those trips up the hill alone. Many people helped me in this effort. Intellectually, the project began while I was a graduate student Columbia University. I wrote a paper for a graduate seminar taught by Ira Katznelson dealing with conceptual issues related to policy substance, the study of Congress, and American political development. Ira was already my dissertation chair at the time (along with Nolan McCarty, who was co-chair), but the paper was a "critical juncture," as it led to a series of collaborations. Those collaborative projects have been instrumental to this book. Specifically, the coding schema in this book is based on our joint work. In addition to being a terrific co-author, Ira has influenced my own work in more ways than seem possible. His intellect and work ethic make him a truly inspiring individual. I owe him a great debt.

Many others deserve credit in the making of this book. Josh Clinton, a frequent co-author, was instrumental in turning my earlier work on measuring legislative significance into much more refined and sophisticated work. The legislative significance measure presented in chapter 4 is based on our collaborative efforts. He is clearly a partner in this project. There are others who also provided much good counsel. One of those individuals is David Mayhew. I had the good fortune to develop a relationship with David during my stint at Yale University. He is a scholar who provides inspiration and much good advice. His social science instincts are unparalleled, and his advice was instrumental for many of the concepts in this book.

There are countless other individuals to thank, including Scott Adler, Richard Bensel, Sean Farhang, Bryan Jones, Nolan McCarty, Sunita Parikh, Keith Poole, Rose Razaghian, Charlie Riemann, Eric Schickler, Wendy Schiller, Robert Shapiro, Stephen Skowronek, Rogers Smith, Charles Stewart, and Greg Wawro. I am also grateful for the workshop participants at Cal Tech, MIT, Columbia, Yale, NYU, and Brown. All served as wonderful audiences for different sections of this book. The National Science Foundation provided much-needed resources to complete the data collection in this book (award #0318280), as did the Institution for Social and Policy Studies at Yale University, the Brown Center at the University of Pennsylvania, and the Russell Sage Foundation's Visiting Scholar Program.

This book required an army of research assistants to help in its making, and some of them were particularly important. David Bateman is a terrific PhD candidate and will soon make a fine professor. His contributions to the casework in this book made him a co-author of chapter 4. Chris Brown is also an amazing graduate student. He is a collaborator of mine in other projects, but his help with this project was instrumental to finishing the book. Many of the earlier research assistants on this project have gone on to become professors at very good institutions or to pursue other fine careers, including Daniel Galvin, Matt Glassman, Christina Greer, Quinn Mulroy, Eldon Porter, and Melanie Springer.

I want to extend a special thanks to Chuck Myers, my editor at Princeton University Press. Chuck is an amazing editor. His guidance and encouragement led to a much better book. His patience is also extraordinary. I also want to thank the two anonymous reviewers: their comments were tough-minded, but again helped me make the book better. I would also like to thank Leslie Grundfest and Eric Henney of Princeton University Press. Finally, I thank my copyeditor Cindy Buck. Her excellent sense of style, combined with a sharp knowledge of the social sciences, made this book sharper and much easier to read. I really cannot believe my luck in being able to work with such a talented group of professionals.

Others have also helped in the writing of this book. The staff of Yale's Institution for Social and Policy Studies, including Pam LaMonaca, Barbara Dozier, Pamela Greene, and Ella Futrell, provided an ideal work environment. They made me feel like I was staying at the Four Seasons Hotel every day.

The book is dedicated to my wife, Anjali Shaw. I would not have finished this book if it were not for her. She has always provided me with constant encouragement and timely advice throughout my career. Her intellectual prowess and no-nonsense approach to life have greatly contributed to any success I have achieved as an academic. In fact, I would not have pursued this career if it were not for her. I owe her a great debt, which will never be fully repaid.

THE SUBSTANCE OF REPRESENTATION

Chapter I

Policy Issue Substance and the Revitalization of Legislative Studies

WHEN LEGISLATIVE STUDIES EXPLODED in the 1960s and 1970s, many scholars took seriously the idea that policy issue substance was theoretically and empirically a very important consideration. During this earlier moment, scholars such as Theodore Lowi (1964, 1970, 1972), Aage Clausen (1967, 1973), David Mayhew (1966), and a young aspiring PhD candidate (and future Congress member and vice president), Richard Cheney (Clausen and Cheney 1970) were curious about how the types and content of issues under discussion shape political behavior and how lawmaking subsequently produces particular policy outputs.[1] At the outset of this fertile period for legislative studies—which would produce tremendous advances in systematic studies of Congress—work privileging policy issue content seemed poised for prominence, perhaps even predominance, within the subfield. The situation would quickly change, however, for reasons explored in this book. By the mid-1980s the substance-centered line of research was nearly nonexistent, and by the 2000s it seemed to have donned a cloak of invisibility.

The complete disappearance of issue substance from the study of policymaking and Congress by Congress scholars leads to two natural questions. First, what was the reason for this disappearance? And second, does it matter? In other words, has the removal of policy issue substance from our study of Congress hindered progress in our understanding of how the lawmaking and policymaking processes work in the United States?

In attempting to answer the second question—which is the central focus of this book—I demonstrate repeatedly, through both theoretical and empirical exercises, that the removal of policy issue substance from our study of Congress has mattered very much and indeed has been extremely costly.

---

[1] Aage Clausen and Richard Cheney (1970) demonstrated the distinct existence and effects of economic and social welfare policy dimensions in roll call voting, hypothesizing that the economic dimension is influenced more by partisan differences and the social welfare dimension by constituency constraints.

The cost of omitting policy substance takes two primary forms. The first is mischaracterization of the policymaking process. Specifically, I show that we often make incorrect inferences about lawmaking when we neglect policy substance. Sometimes these mistakes in assessing theories of lawmaking and/or policymaking lead us to lump laws together by issue area in our analyses rather than considering them separately. For example, an empirical regularity that we believe to be true (and that therefore might serve as a cornerstone for future theory building) may be contingent on aggregating all policy types together; that "regularity" changes or even disappears once we disaggregate policies by issue type. A concrete example can be found in the literature on congressional polarization, which is built around two empirical findings that are now treated as facts: that polarization has been increasing since the 1970s, and that polarization has followed a U-shaped form across the last 130 years of American history (McCarty, Poole, and Rosenthal 2006). These two empirical findings have driven theoretical and empirical research on polarization, but as I show later in this book, they do not hold across policy issue areas. In reality, the polarization story is a much more complex one after policy issue substance is introduced into the equation.

There are consequences for getting it only partially right, or even wrong. In the case of the polarization literature, introducing a more accurate picture of how polarization behaves across policy issue areas could reshape the theoretical literature on the topic. I show here that domestic politics is almost always highly polarized, but that the pattern changes in the realm of international relations and sovereignty policy. These divergent findings call for a rethinking of polarization. This point is not, of course, confined to the study of elite polarization.[2] Regardless of whether our efforts are aimed at testing theories or empirically attempting to understand patterns in policymaking, not taking policy issue substance into consideration repeatedly leads us into making incorrect inferences and statements about lawmaking. Simply put, omitting policy substance makes us get it wrong, and getting it wrong is extremely costly for many reasons, given what is at stake. Fifteen years ago, Charles Jones (1995, 1) made this point about the costs of getting lawmaking wrong in his presidential address to the American Political Science Association:

> Lawmaking is the core decision-making process of a democratic state. It is the means for defining, promoting, and regulating community life and, accordingly, is spectacularly interesting and highly relevant to our purposes as political scientists.

---

[2] "Elite polarization" is the term for professional politicians differentiating or separating themselves along party lines.

Thus, a critical endeavor for political scientists is to arrive at clear and accurate understandings, characterizations, and explanations of the lawmaking process. The lessons of Jones's address are no less relevant today than when he delivered it. I argue throughout this book that we will never get lawmaking right without seriously bringing policy issue substance into our study of it.

The second cost of omitting policy issue substance as a topic of study is less obvious and also more difficult to prove. I argue that this omission has sequestered congressional studies from other subfields—particularly American political development (APD) and to a lesser extent policy studies—primarily because both are interested directly in what Congress scholars for the most part no longer study: issue-specific policy outputs.[3] I also suggest that this sequestering of the Congress subfield is an important reason why it has lost its place as the most theoretically and empirically interesting area of political science. This is not to say that the Congress subfield is not still producing interesting research. Instead, I argue that policy issue substance is the key for the subfield to make another significant advancement in our understanding of how Congress behaves as well as how lawmaking works. Policy issue substance is the key to new progress.

Although there are certainly many reasons why the Congress subfield is not directly engaged with the APD subfield and policy studies, and vice versa, the omission of policy issue substance is probably the most important reason (see Katznelson and Lapinski 2006a). The direct cost of not having Congress scholars engaged with APD and policy studies is, of course, impossible to fully determine. How do we determine what we would know about policymaking if there was synergy between these subfields? Fortunately, this question is one that can be partially set aside: it is axiomatic that having three diverse and talented groups of scholars attempting to better understand policymaking would lead to a much better overall understanding. This question must not, however, be fully avoided. The next section considers not only the contribution of APD and policy studies to congressional studies, but also the potential revitalization of these two subfields by restoring to them the study of policy issue substance in lawmaking.

Before discussing the path by which we might bring policy substance back into the study of Congress and lawmaking—with the goal of providing better inferences and predictions about lawmaking while building synergy between Congress, APD, and policy scholars—I take a closer look at why policy substance is no longer a part of congressional studies, what has been lost as a result, and why we need to bring it back.

---

[3] Why have Congress scholars avoided the study of lawmaking, particularly issue-specific lawmaking? Jones (1995, 2) surmises that "the study of laws is bound to be issue-specific and will be marked by the dreaded label case study, with its limited potential for theory."

WHY WE NEED TO RESTORE POLICY ISSUE SUBSTANCE TO CONGRESSIONAL STUDIES

There is, of course, no single explanation for why policy substance is no longer an important consideration in our study of Congress. One explanation points to the rising prominence of deductive theory within congressional studies: behavior work on policy substance dwindled as scholars began to think of it as limited to descriptive objectives (Katznelson and Lapinski 2006a). In a related development, the powerful work of Keith Poole and Howard Rosenthal (1985; 1991; 1997) has demonstrated empirically that roll call voting in the U.S. Congress appears to be largely unidimensional. An even more important finding of Poole and Rosenthal's for the disappearance of policy substance from the study of Congress is that members' preferences measured through roll call voting do not vary much issue by issue. Although Poole and Rosenthal's work on this specific topic is limited, the mountain of empirical findings they have produced on the low dimensionality of the political issue space has encouraged most Congress scholars to conflate low dimensionality with the idea that policy issue substance is inconsequential. Why is it so unfortunate that their forceful results have provided a mistaken empirical foundation to the argument that studying policy issue substance is not necessary to understand the behavior of members of Congress or policymaking in the United States? Because low dimensionality does not imply that members' preferences across issue areas are more or less the same. I insist throughout the book that these two issues, low dimensionality and policy issue substance, should be separated.

It is somewhat paradoxical to argue that the omission of policy substance from our congressional studies has been costly when that omission coincides with a remarkably fertile period in the history of such studies. From roughly the mid-1980s until a pinnacle in the early 2000s, congressional studies produced important and rigorous findings that have fundamentally changed our understanding of Congress. The bulk of this period's work focused on why institutions, rules, and procedures are formed and how they influence collective choice. The theory building in congressional studies during this period was supplemented by careful empirical evaluations, and the majority of the hypotheses derived or constructed made empirical predictions that related to political behavior, not to policy outputs.[4]

The study of Congress through roll call votes has a long and rich history in political science. There is certainly nothing wrong with studying the political behavior of members of Congress, and there is no question that roll call voting records provide an excellent way to do so. However, with so many scholars engaged in this institutionally based work on Congress, the direct study of

---

[4]There are some notable exceptions, especially in historically oriented work (see Brady 1988).

policy outputs has been left to others. Moreover, the study of political behavior with no counterbalancing focus on outputs may have been unhealthy for both the study of lawmaking and the subfield of Congress studies.

This began to change after the publication of David Mayhew's *Divided We Govern* (1991). Mayhew demonstrated the importance of moving beyond an orientation toward rules, institutions, and procedures in studying the behavior of members of Congress and focusing instead on explaining what government does. His seminal work brought the study of policy outputs back into congressional studies, spurring the creation of a small cottage industry that assesses the legislative performance of Congress.[5] This work has collectively increased our understanding of the determinants of lawmaking (see Adler and Lapinski 2006; Binder 1999, 2003; Coleman 1999; McCarty, Poole, and Rosenthal 2006), although it has remained silent on the question of whether policy substance is an important causal factor in lawmaking.

Even though we know more today about the determinants of lawmaking than ever before, much remains unknown. This limited understanding has been attributed by some to the near-invisibility of policy issue substance in our research (Katznelson and Lapinski 2006b; Lapinski 2008; Rohde 1991).[6] Evidence that the omission of policy substance is hindering rather than helping our understanding of lawmaking can be found in some fine recent empirical assessments of theoretical models of lawmaking in the United States.

The two most prominent models of this type are the "pivotal politics" model of lawmaking (Brady and Volden 1998; Krehbiel 1998) and the "party cartel" model (Cox and McCubbins 2005).[7] The pivotal politics model of lawmaking predicts that policy change occurs when status-quo policies are extreme relative to the preferences of members of Congress. More specifically, a gridlock interval can be constructed by examining key "pivots" in the separation-of-powers system. These pivots are defined by the filibuster in the Senate (the cloture pivot) and the presidential veto.[8] Policy change occurs

---

[5]There is in fact a body of early work that considered the importance of policy outputs. See, for example, Chamberlain (1946). See also the issues of the American Political Science Review (vol. 14, no. 1, to vol. 41, no. 4, 1919–1949) and Political Science Quarterly (vol. 17, no. 4, to vol. 26, no. 04, 1887–1925) summarize legislative activity in Congress.

[6]David Rohde (1991, 357) wrote a little over a decade ago that "the challenge for students of congressional politics is . . . not to prove that one theoretical view is superior in all situations but instead to specify the conditions under which each view applies to behavior and outcomes of interest."

[7]The "conditional party government" model (Aldrich and Rohde 2000; Aldrich 1995) is another alternative account of lawmaking. This prominent model differs from the party cartel model by critically linking the ability of the majority party to pass policy with the homogeneity of the preferences of the majority party. A homogeneous party is one that can agree on policy change, and thus one that is more likely to be productive in passing legislation.

[8]How the interval is constructed depends on the preferences of the president and members of Congress. See Krehbiel (1998).

precisely when the status quo of an existing policy is extreme relative to the gridlock interval. Like the pivotal politics model, the party cartel model of lawmaking also constructs a gridlock interval, but it differs in that the gridlock interval depends on the preferences of the median members of the majority party and the chamber median.[9] In both models, policy change is determined by the location of status-quo policies relative to the preferences of critical members of Congress.

As mentioned, empirical assessments of these formal models of lawmaking have been less than stellar. For example, in a well-executed test of the pivotal politics, party cartel, and median voter models of lawmaking, Keith Krehbiel, Adam Meirowitz, and Jonathan Woon 2005 summarize their overall findings as "painfully inconclusive."[10] They propose two possible explanations for their lackluster empirical results: either the theoretical models were wrong or the empirical tests were flawed. A lack of attention to policy substance may play a large role in either explanation.

The first possible explanation for why theoretical models of lawmaking do not receive strong empirical affirmation may be rooted in policy content. This would be the case if the mechanisms underlying policymaking vary by policy issue substance (Lapinski 2008; Rohde 1991). The idea here is that different processes explain lawmaking across policy issue domains. The task therefore is to identify how mechanisms vary according to policy substance.[11] To understand how these mechanisms work, we need to get a firm grasp on the empirical regularities of lawmaking across policy issues and time periods. This understanding, in turn, will allow us to determine the strengths and weaknesses of our theoretical models.

The second explanation proposed by Krehbiel and his colleagues (2005) for the poor fit between theory and data, the issue of measurement, is also linked to policy substance. Scholars believe that inconclusive empirical results stem from improperly measuring the induced preferences of members of Congress that are needed to assess existing models. In other words, problematic empirical results are not a result of poor models, but of the poor measures used to test the models. This is the explanation favored by Krehbiel and his colleagues

---

[9] See Cox and McCubbins (2005) for details.

[10] According to Krehbiel and his colleagues (2005, 17), "a series of indirect test results were painfully inconclusive.... While this analysis suggests somewhat more convincingly that gridlock-based theories provide marginal value over median voter theory, their marginal value over the random-normal null model is questionable."

[11] This idea is not new, and in fact it was first seriously introduced by Theodore Lowi (1964, 688) over forty years ago when he argued that we need to better understand how "a political relationship is determined by the type of policy at stake, so that for every policy there is likely to be a distinctive type of political relationship." Lowi's policy classification system, though suggestive, proved too abstract and difficult to operationalize and thus was never widely adopted within congressional studies.

for the lackluster results of their study. They believe that the empirical results for their pivotal politics model of lawmaking would improve if the induced preferences of members of Congress were measured by policy issue area. Their belief, in short, is that induced policy preferences vary by policy issue domain. Not accounting for variation by policy substance leads to measurement error and therefore attenuated (weak) results.[12]

This book contends that policy issue substance is at the center of the poor results found by Krehbiel and his colleagues. Assessing their idea in more detail, we can examine how the assumptions underlying these two models of lawmaking might interact with policy issue substance. Empirical evaluations of the pivotal politics and party cartel models make specific implicit assumptions to produce testable predictions for legislative accomplishment across time. Many of the nonformal theories of lawmaking discussed earlier also make these assumptions, which have to do with the desire and opportunity to pass legislation.

The first assumption is that all legislative regimes are equally interested in legislating. At least one scholar has made the case that not all legislative regimes are alike. John Coleman (1999) argues that Democrats are more likely than Republicans to enact new legislation when they control government. This type of assumption is not fully explored in most preference-based models of lawmaking. Instead, most scholars assume that lawmakers would like to enact or move policies closer to their ideal points regardless of their ideological positioning.[13]

The second assumption about the opportunity to pass legislation is particularly critical for models of lawmaking that construct gridlock intervals. Empirical assessments of such models require that gridlock intervals, which have been constructed from electoral and roll call data, be highly correlated with the number of movable status quos. The usual assumption is that the distribution of movable status-quo points is uniform across the policy space. A uniform distribution is highly desirable because it ensures that change in

---

[12]In speculating that their lackluster findings are related to the absence of policy substance from their empirical analyses, Krehbiel and his colleagues (2005) specifically suspect the lack of disaggregating roll calls by policy issue area as the culprit in improper measurement of the induced preferences of members of Congress for their theoretical testing. They write: "Unidimensional theories assume only that preferences exist and are well behaved on a single dimension in any given choice situation. They do not assume, as does the implementation of tests of the sort we conducted, that well-defined preferences of Senators maintain the same orderings and locations on the same primary dimension across all roll calls" (17, emphasis in original). In other words, their intuition is that the ordering of senators varies by policy issue substance.

[13]Most current work on lawmaking does not consider problematic the assumption that all legislatures (or parties) want to pass legislation. Robert Erikson, Michael Mackuen, and James Stimson (2002) show, however, that liberal-tilting major enactments outnumber conservative enactments nine to one (for a discussion of this point, see Mayhew 2006).

predicted legislative accomplishment is not dependent on the location of the pivots being changed. The intuitive idea behind this assumption is that an equal change in the gridlock interval width should have the same effect on lawmaking, regardless of whether the change occurs in a moderate section of the issue space or in a more extreme portion. The problem with this assumption is that the distribution of movable status quos is unlikely to be uniform (or even normal) but is in fact probably quite lumpy across time, particularly across different policy issue areas.

Mayhew's (2005a; 2005b) most recent work fleshes out much of the intuition about why policy substance and the distribution of movable status quos are likely to be related. He argues that events such as wars, economic crises, and assassinations are important factors that drive policy change. Why do such events matter for lawmaking? In his work, Mayhew leverages the research of others, primarily John Kingdon's (1984) writings on "policy windows," which suggest that crises alter the demand and supply of public policies. Another way of expressing this is that crises often delegitimize existing government policies that are directly or, indirectly linked to the specific event. Consequently, a crisis can immediately shift the distribution of movable status-quo policies for linked policies. This type of shift can and usually does happen quickly. The most recent and immediate example is the post–September 11, 2001, 107th Congress.[14]

Mayhew argues that there are long- and short-term effects of crises and other major events on policymaking. In his article on war, he constructs lists of legislation that would not have come into existence if specific wars in American history had not been fought. Crises and war therefore can rapidly change the status-quo locations of policies linked to such events. Mayhew's (2005b, 36) own words best explain this intuition.

> To use the terms presented by Keith Krehbiel in *Pivotal Politics*, it is not just elections that are capable of moving status quo policy outside the Capitol Hill "gridlock interval." Events, too, can shake up a preference distribution among the realm of elected officeholders to the point where presidential vetoes, Senate filibusters and the rest cease to be a bar to action in some direction. Let me nail this down with an instance. On December 7, 1941, Pearl Harbor was attacked. On December 8, 1941, Congress and the president opted to abandon the American status quo of not waging war against Japan, and war was declared.

The status-quo policies that are affected by a crisis are not random. Instead, they are linked by policy substance to the event itself. For example, in the case of war, international affairs issues, including defense policies that are

---

[14]Mayhew (2006, 248) makes this point by listing sixteen important enactments for the 107th Congress, nine of which were a part of the government's response to the 9/11 attack.

classified as international affairs, as well as war-related domestic policies have movable status quos that were not likely to have been movable immediately prior to the event unless a major change in the gridlock interval resulted because of electoral replacement. An event such as war will not necessarily change the perception and location of status-quo policies across all policy types. Thus, policy substance enters the equation. Crises can change the distribution of movable status-quo points for certain types or groups of policy.[15]

It has thus been demonstrated that it is quite possible, if not likely, that crises and other significant events by themselves can shift the distributions of movable status quos for different policy issues. Some policies might be quite immune to change, however, because they are not linked to the event. The problem with pooled analysis of lawmaking is that the analysis might not pick up such effects, depending on which and how many policies are affected by such shocks. This example simply calls attention to the fact that different mechanisms might drive lawmaking within substantive issue areas. Empirically, chapter 6 explores in more detail the ideas put forward here about the determinants of legislative performance.

It is also possible to argue that policy issue substance matters for measuring the political preferences of members of Congress. This is a belief that informed the earlier Congress literature on political behavior. For example, if instead of moving distributions of status quos, events actually change the preferences of members, policy substance is equally important because the induced preferences of members are likely to be changed for some policies but not others. There are other good theoretical reasons to expect differences by issue area, depending on the salience of each issue (see, for example, Arnold 1990).

Let's consider a specific example of how members of Congress might have distinct preferences across issue areas. One of the issue categories introduced later in the coding schema employed throughout this book is sovereignty policy, which is concerned with the boundaries of a state's internal authority and the content of the citizenship regime linking the state and a diverse population. With only a few exceptions, scholars in American

---

[15]Krehbiel (1998) and Cox and McCubbins (2005) discuss the possible influence of exogenous shocks on the location of status-quo policies. In his chapter on coalition size, Krehbiel (1998, 78) writes:

> Unlike election-induced preference shocks, status quo shocks may occur at any time, including within periods that are demarcated by elections. A cause might be new information that suddenly becomes available and that alters the lawmakers' perceptions about attributes associated with old policies.... Only rarely is it possible to predict or observe precisely when such changes occur.

Cox and McCubbins (2005) argue that the location of status-quo points is a function of policy in the previous time period and of exogenous shocks.

politics have had little explicit interest in sovereignty policy. In particular, the policy has had no analytical traction for Congress scholars, most of whom would lump issues of sovereignty into the category of domestic politics. There is, however, an emerging literature in American constitutional development that has paid closer attention to the differences between sovereignty policy and other policy issue areas. This literature, relatively unknown to Congress scholars, provides important motivation for students of Congress interested in member behavior or lawmaking to consider sovereignty issues separately. It also provides evidence that members of Congress may have very distinct preferences on sovereignty issues compared to other policy categories.

The American constitutional development literature argues that sovereignty policy is unique in the American context because, beginning in the late nineteenth century and continuing today, the Supreme Court has decided that "Congress [has] plenary power to construct the American state and its membership largely immune from judicial review" in cases concerning federal authority over immigrants, Indian nations, and territorial governance—all key aspects of sovereignty policy (Cleveland 2002, 11; Aleinikoff 2002). In deciding that Congress has plenary power to regulate the entry of aliens, the status of the Indian nations, the acquisition of territory, and the admission of states into the Union, "the courts would not subject congressional choices to any limitations on federal power located elsewhere in the constitution (such as the First Amendment or the prohibition against retroactive legislation)" (Aleinikoff 2002, 16). Given the central role of Congress in the formulation of sovereignty policy, the relative lack of attention to it by congressional scholars is striking.[16]

The dominance of Congress in these issue areas is likely to have changed the dynamics of lawmaking in complicated ways. For one, the stakes of lawmaking have probably been higher, given the foreclosure of alternative avenues for modifying or overturning legislation and the difficulty of substantially modifying existing laws in Congress. At the extreme, statehood is effectively locked in after Congress has admitted a territory into the Union. Immigration law, Indian policy, and territorial governance are unlikely to be overturned by the Court, and although the Court continues to review administrative actions in these areas, it has not significantly challenged congressional plenary power. This may have had important effects on legislator behavior, especially if encouraging the judicialization of an issue has been an

---

[16]The judiciary is much more active in the realm of civil rights and liberties. Nevertheless, in some areas of civil rights, and in voting rights in particular, the Court has tended during the last several decades to support Congress's assertion of extraordinary power.

important strategy for political leaders to avoid fracturing their political coalitions (Graber 1993).

More broadly, the content of sovereignty policy suggests that it is the site of politics that do not map onto the dominant ideological cleavage. Sovereignty policy is more likely to be concerned with the "background conditions" of national life—who are the people, and over what territory does the state govern—than with proximate questions of economic redistribution and regulation. The prospects of changed citizenship and territory are likely to alter the preferences and relative positions of political actors in complex ways. If nothing else, changes to territory and citizenship could heighten tensions among existing political coalitions. New territories, bringing in new issues and voters or an expanded or contracted suffrage, might alter the scope of conflict and create new cleavages that destabilize existing coalitions. As noted by Daniel Tichenor (2002, 8) in regard to the politics of U.S. immigration policy—a key area of sovereignty—the political dynamics "have long been influenced by the making and remaking of distinctive political coalitions on this issue that cut across familiar partisan and ideological lines." Even where the boundaries of membership are not being expanded or restricted, sovereignty policy is often concerned with strongly held beliefs about civic identities. Infringements on free speech, the place of religion in American society, and the civic status and equality of citizens are debates that engage beliefs about what it means to be a citizen of a state, and these beliefs are not likely to correspond neatly with the party structure. They may correspond to sectional, religious, and regional identities, or they may be much more idiosyncratic preferences.

For all of these reasons, members of Congress are likely to hold preferences in sovereignty policy that differ from their preferences in many other issue areas. Of course, this literature does not give us strong expectations about the impact of specific member behavior on sovereignty policy. In fact, it does very much the opposite. How these conflicts and altered dynamics play out is historically contingent and depends on how a specific policy interacts with existing coalitional arrangements and member preferences. Nor should we homogenize sovereignty policy or imply that its different dimensions function in the same way. What is likely, however, is that preferences on sovereignty policy will not map onto the dominant issue cleavages of a given period, and so there is good reason to attempt to measure the preferences of sovereignty policy separately for members. A good example of what Krehbiel, Meirowitz, and Woon (2005) were talking about, sovereignty policy shows us why we should take policy issue substance into account when measuring the preferences of members of Congress. The full costs of aggregating roll call votes to study lawmaking are explored systematically in chapters 3 and 4. Here it is sufficient to point out that this is a potentially large problem to which very little attention has been given.

A NATURAL CONNECTION: CONGRESSIONAL STUDIES, AMERICAN POLITICAL DEVELOPMENT, AND POLICY STUDIES

Bringing policy issue substance back to the study of Congress would certainly improve our overall understanding of lawmaking, but how might the study of Congress and lawmaking benefit scholars of American political development? And what specifically might APD scholars bring to the study of congressional policymaking? Before turning to these questions, we should note that APD, though still young as a subfield, has many accomplishments to its credit already, but very few are related to the study of Congress. Congress studies, in fact, have never been integrated into APD (Katznelson and Lapinski 2006a; Lapinski 2000; Whittington 1999), whose focus has been elsewhere, including the pursuit of more and better work on American political history than has been achieved by much of the history profession (especially during the long period, now coming to a close, when political studies were avoided by younger political historians). APD scholars have also contributed a great deal to the growing interest in historical evidence and dynamics on the part of their political science colleagues who are otherwise inclined to deductive modeling and large-N studies. Notwithstanding these achievements, APD currently faces a central problem: the subfield's distinct purposes have become less clearly defined (Katznelson and Lapinski 2006a).

The APD subfield is at a crossroads partially because of its own success. APD effectively advanced analytical political history when historians of the United States were turning away from political subjects and political scientists were seeking to identify behavioral regularities or distinguish portable models of strategic action without much regard for the singular traits of specific times and places. Perhaps unfortunately, the APD subfield's monopoly on interesting political history has ended. Many historians, especially talented younger scholars, have taken a decided turn back to politics and the state, while a growing (though still small) number of Americanists in political science have learned the lesson of APD that history is integral to good causal scholarship. Paradoxically, by encouraging the return of historians to political history and prompting an attention to historical questions on the part of other students of American politics, the APD subfield now is under pressure to better explain how its own qualities validate its continued contributions at the intersection of history and political science.

While there is, of course, more than one promising direction that might be taken to move the APD subfield forward and bring its special qualities to bear on a wider arc of issues and institutions, this book advances a path that advocates bringing Congress to the center of APD, although this effort cannot succeed without some decisive moves. The best way forward for a serious engagement between Congress scholars and APD scholars should be one based on a robust and systematic approach to studying the policy issue content of lawmaking. In other words, policy substance can be used to make Congress a constitutive feature of the analysis of the most important APD questions. In order for this to work, the study of lawmaking must draw on policy issue content that makes sense to APD scholars. The lack of a theoretically grounded and empirically useful policy issue classification system has been a major stumbling block for integrating Congress and lawmaking systematically into the study of APD. This book introduces the tools necessary to integrate APD into this work on its own terms.

APD, in turn, could help Congress scholars by continuing to bring important and needed historical perspective to the study of Congress and by helping Congress scholars make conscious connections between their work and the larger overarching themes that are important to the American regime. Specifically, APD scholars have primarily worked in four genres: exploring critical periods; steering critical subjects through key moments in, or even the whole of, American political history; tracing the development of key institutions, in both the medium and long terms; and exploring political speech and ideas. Within these genres, APD scholars have developed a few substantive themes, including liberalism, state building, temporalism, and policy feedback (see Katznelson and Lapinski 2006a). Congress scholars rarely make the connection between these APD themes and ideas, although clear linkages exist. For example, representation, a concept of perennial importance to Congress scholars, has a clear relationship to liberalism, but that connection is ignored within almost all Congress scholarship.

In summary, the themes that define APD as a distinct subfield are rarely, if ever, engaged by Congress scholars, to the detriment of legislative studies. Specifically, Congress scholars, in giving no attention to these themes, find themselves unable to join the conversation about central questions concerning the American regime and unable to build specific historical knowledge about timing and context into their models of policymaking. It is one purpose of this book to show that ideas distinctive to APD studies can be used to gain a better understanding of Congress and policymaking.

Although APD would benefit and assist congressional studies by turning attention to the study of policy substance and lawmaking, it is also true that policy studies reconnected to congressional studies would be similarly beneficial and contribute to our understanding of lawmaking. It is paradoxical that a divide exists between the two subfields at all, since at one time policy studies and political science worked in close tandem (and in fact were essentially indistinguishable). In earlier times, influential crossover work focused on "the mechanics of agenda change, the likelihood of nonincremental policy change, and how the policy-making process varies across issue areas"(Gormley 2007, 297). The divide that now exists between policy studies and political science is manifested in several ways. Policy studies scholars publish in their own journals, and Congress scholars rarely read or interact with this work.[17] Policy schools, including those that focus on public administration and policy more generally, have concentrated their faculty hiring in the field of economics, and some prefer "practitioners in the field." In short, the alliance between policy studies and political science today is clearly weak, and only a few notable scholars work between the two fields.[18]

Much might be gained in policy studies and political science if the two fields were to rejoin forces. For example, policy studies scholars, particularly economists, are very interested in exploring the consequences of public policy choices, while political scientists have spent very little energy on this topic (Gormley 2007, 298).[19] This lack of attention is unfortunate considering that past policy choices clearly have a huge impact on the policymaking process. Because past policy choices are specific to particular policy domains, policy substance, again, might serve as a bridge between policy studies and political science and help both disciplines gain a better understanding of how policymaking works.

THE ORGANIZATION OF THE BOOK

The purpose of this book is to reintroduce a substance-oriented research program based on policy issues for studying Congress from multiple vantage points. In doing so, my aim is to make serious progress on systematically understanding Lowi's provocative claim that "policy determines politics," which, while important, has never been satisfactorily understood, either empirically or theoretically. The bulk of this book tackles this question empirically, though there is, of course, plenty of theoretical discussion on how to best construct a proper categorization schema as well as how to construct appropriate measures of political preferences and legislative productivity.

In advancing a substance-oriented approach to studying policymaking and lawmaking in Congress, this book introduces a kit bag of important new tools and ideas to use in determining how policy issue substance matters for lawmaking, including: new data, such as an immense data set on U.S. lawmaking between 1877 to 1994; new and massive measures of political

---

[17]Whether policy studies scholars keep up with work within the Congress subfield is unclear (see Gormley 2007).

[18]The most visible scholars working within both fields are Frank Baumgartner and Bryan Jones (1993, 2004), whose work clearly falls within the policy studies tradition and who have produced the most powerful analytical framework and empirical work on the subject. Nevertheless, their work, which focuses primarily on how issues become a part of the political agenda, nearly stands alone as important work that informs both political scientists and policy studies scholars.

[19]Keith Krehbiel's (1991) informational theory is a significant exception. An important assumption of informational theory is that politicians are uncertain about policy outcomes.

preferences broken down by policy issue areas for U.S. lawmakers spanning the period 1877 to 2010; and fresh approaches to analyzing these new data sets. The book is predicated on the idea that new and improved data are needed to make additional progress in understanding lawmaking.

The book is organized into seven chapters. Chapter 2, "Bringing Policy Issue Substance Back In," has two purposes. The chapter's title draws a parallel to the famous edited volume *Bringing the State Back In* (Evans, Rueschemeyer, and Skocpol 1985), which many scholars believe spurred the creation of American political development as a distinct subfield of political science. Similarly, policy issue substance could play a revitalizing role for multiple subfields in American politics, particularly congressional studies and American political development. The second chapter builds on some of the ideas that have been briefly introduced here in chapter 1, namely, why policy issue substance disappeared from the study of Congress and what is needed to revive this approach. I begin chapter 2 by arguing that three factors combined to lessen interest in the study of policy substance: the rise of deductive theory within congressional studies, which led scholars to believe that this earlier behavior-based work was limited to descriptive objectives; the findings of Poole and Rosenthal (1985, 1991, 1997), who demonstrated empirically that roll call voting in the U.S. Congress appears to be largely unidimensional and not policy-specific; and policy classification schemas that were not theoretically grounded and suffered from being period-bound.

The second and primary purpose of chapter 2, however, is to introduce and explain a new coding schema to parse policy. This coding schema is without question the most important part of the book. By returning to and advancing the key intuition that the content of policymaking matters, I seek to overcome the specification and measurement problems that have plagued past researchers. Picking up where others have stopped, I identify and clear the most important theoretical and empirical roadblock that has stood in the way of the substantive policy research program: the absence of a sufficiently compelling, analytically directed, and theoretically supported method for coding the content of congressional roll calls and public laws and, in consequence, the lack of a data set across American history that records both the behavior of members and the legislative output they generate organized by such a classification approach. The schema introduced here differs considerably from past policy classification systems in that its categories are heavily motivated by theoretical work within the American political development subfield. I explain the schema in detail, including its theoretical justifications, and include a brief descriptive analysis of the roll call and lawmaking data used throughout the later chapters.

Chapter 3, "Political Polarization and Issues: A New Perspective," details the ways in which policy issue substance matters for studying political preferences and is the first of four empirical chapters in the book. Fully exploring how policy issue substance matters for studying political polarization in Congress, the chapter begins by introducing a new large data set that comprises the estimated induced preferences of members of the House of Representatives and U.S. senators by policy issue area over a very long time horizon—1877 to 2010. Overall, the data set includes 28,196 ideal point estimates for House members as well as 6,652 estimates of political preferences for senators.

The second section of the chapter explores the literature on elite polarization in Congress by policy issue area and studies polarization across a 124-year period (1877 to 2010) by the policy issue areas defined as "tier 1" (the most basic four types of state policy adjudicated by modern democratic legislatures). Here I demonstrate empirically that issue content is extremely important for understanding political polarization and that many of the empirical "facts" about polarization depend on not disaggregating policy by issue areas. The research presented suggests that we have much to learn about how and why polarization varies so much by issue content.

Chapter 4, "The Case Studies: Policy Issue Substance and the Political Behavior of Members of Congress," details the ways in which policy issue substance matters for studying political preferences at the micro level. The first section of chapter 4 reconsiders Poole and Rosenthal's analysis of the 95th Congress (1977–78). In their analysis of the 95th Congress, which happened during President Jimmy Carter's first term, they ask: do different issues give different scales? They find evidence they interpret to mean that issue scales do not vary. I present evidence to suggest that this is not correct: it is possible to agree wholeheartedly with the low-dimensionality findings of Poole and Rosenthal, but at the same time, as I show, members of Congress have distinct preferences across policy issue areas. Measuring the preferences of members of Congress correctly is absolutely vital for empirical testing of theories and hypotheses as well as for inductive-based work on lawmaking. I argue that this is not possible to do without including policy issue substance in the picture.

The last section of chapter 4 presents five case studies of lawmaking, from five different Congresses. I selected these cases, which focus on issues of notable lawmaking within the tier 1 issue category of sovereignty, to maximize temporal diversity: each is from a different historical period in American political development. The case studies show in a more fine-grained manner the impact of policy preferences across time and issues.

In chapter 5, "Legislative Accomplishment and Policy Issue Substance," I introduce a new measure of legislative accomplishment. At the center of this book lies an ambitious empirical effort to better understand how policy substance is important for lawmaking. To understand lawmaking requires that we move beyond studying political behavior in Congress alone and beyond a complete empirical reliance on roll call votes. Roll calls are invaluable for studying the behavior of members and certain components of lawmaking. But we also need appropriate direct measures of legislative outputs.

Legislative behavior and legislative outputs must be studied in tandem to gain a proper understanding of the lawmaking process in the United States. Unfortunately, the lack of measures that capture legislative accomplishment, especially across a long time horizon (including the period prior to World War II), is perhaps the primary reason why we know less than we should about lawmaking in the United States (Brady and Cooper 1981). In chapter 5, I explain the value of studying more important or notable legislation (Krehbiel 1998; Cameron 2000; Clinton and Lapinski 2006). Although the idea of studying important lawmaking across time is not controversial, constructing an appropriate measure is not a trivial exercise. This chapter conceptualizes and constructs a comprehensive lawmaking data set that provides measures of legislative accomplishment at the aggregate level as well as by specific policy issue areas for a 118-year period. This data set will ultimately facilitate the study of lawmaking by giving us the data necessary to significantly improve our empirical understanding of lawmaking and policymaking in the United States.

The first section of chapter 5 describes the type of data we need to better test current theories of congressional lawmaking and provide an empirical spine to some important questions that are central to APD. I present the case for using direct measures of legislative accomplishment based on actual lawmaking data rather than roll call–based measures, which are indirect measures of lawmaking, even if they are the measures most commonly used by Congress scholars.

The second section of chapter 5 provides a detailed account of the conceptualization and estimation of an individual law–level estimate of legislative significance or notability for each of the 37,766 public statutes enacted between 1877 and 1994 (see Clinton and Lapinski 2006). I provide empirical evidence demonstrating that the data have strong face validity.

The third section provides the hinge between the individual significance estimates and the construction of a new measure of legislative accomplishment. Here I explain the construction of Congress-by-Congress measures of legislative accomplishment, including measures broken down by the policy-coding schema.

Chapter 6, "Explaining Lawmaking in the United States, 1877–1994," turns to lawmaking and shows that legislative productivity varies considerably by policy issue area. Specifically, the chapter shows that the key determinants of legislative productivity differ by policy substance, and it provides empirical evidence that questions the benefits of pooling legislation when such aggregation often obscures empirical findings related to understanding the mechanisms of lawmaking.

Through simple correlation analysis as well as multivariate analysis, chapter 6 explores empirically how the measures of legislative performance constructed in chapter 5 behave. The idea is to show variations in policy outputs by issue area and explore the determinants that explain overall legislative performance versus performance in particular policy areas.

The empirical core of this chapter—the multivariate analysis—aims to determine whether pooling policies (using an overall aggregate measure of all legislation) is potentially inappropriate. In other words, when the determinants of lawmaking are analyzed, are important relationships masked or dampened when policy types are pooled instead of disaggregated? This multivariate analysis draws on data using two different thresholds of significance. The highest threshold uses the top 500 enactments—a measure of which is nearly equivalent to the list of landmark enactments produced by David Mayhew in *Divided We Govern* (1991), except that the measure used here covers an additional thirty-five Congresses (over seventy years). The second threshold uses the top 3,500 enactments. This threshold captures landmarks for very important legislation. The multivariate analysis does not include every possible explanation and related covariate in the model because, with fifty-nine Congresses (the unit of measure) in the 118-year period, doing so would lead quickly to a saturated specification and no degree of freedom.

Instead, by presenting a parsimonious specification that includes the most common and important covariates found in the literature, I am able to show repeatedly through this analysis how policy substance matters by comparing the results from the pooled and nonpooled dependent variables. This chapter also draws on the issue-specific measures of polarization introduced in chapter 3 to show how we can better understand legislative productivity if we correctly measure elite political polarization.

In conclusion, chapter 7, "At the Crossroads: Policy Issue Substance, Congress, and American Political Development," builds on the analysis in the previous chapters. I make a final case that policy issue substance is critical for understanding contemporary and historical lawmaking. The conclusion also returns to the importance of studying policy content to any substantial progress we may hope to achieve in congressional studies and American political development.

Chapter II

Bringing Policy Issue Substance Back In

OVER THE LAST THREE DECADES, the study of lawmaking has become dominated by "lumpers"—those who aggregate data and attempt to assess the bigger picture—instead of "splitters," who care most about the particulars of lawmaking.[1] When congressional studies took off in the 1960s and 1970s, splitters dominated the study of Congress and lawmaking. During this earlier moment, scholars were curious about how the types and content of issues shape political behavior and, in turn, how lawmaking works to produce particular policy outputs. Unfortunately, this substance-centered work ended prematurely before realizing its full potential.[2] As deductive theory gained prominence within congressional studies, this behavioral work began to fade because scholars considered it nontheoretical and limited primarily to descriptive objectives.

This chapter focuses on returning to the study of policy issue substance as the best way to improve our understanding of Congress and American political development (APD). The first section reviews the role of the substantive tradition as well as the alternative lines of research (primarily Poole and Rosenthal 1985, 1991, 1997) in the eclipse of the substantive issue–based tradition within congressional studies. If we are to revitalize an issue-centered political science, it is prudent to learn from past limitations of substance-centered work and make corrections when possible. The second section introduces the theoretically derived coding schema to classify both actual legislation and roll call votes by policy area that serves as the cornerstone for the empirical work throughout the book. In this section, I explain the rationale and theoretical framework of my schema.

---

[1]Some of the material in this chapter is adapted or excerpted from Katznelson and Lapinski (2006a, 2006b).

[2]This is not meant to imply that deductive modeling has hindered progress in the pursuit of understanding how Congress works; indeed, the opposite is more often the case. See Krehbiel (1998), chapter 1, for an excellent discussion of the benefits of formal modeling.

PITFALLS OF THE SUBSTANTIVE TRADITION

A chief goal of this book is to revive the substantive research program with stronger conceptual and empirical bases as an integral part of, rather than an alternative to, more recent trends in the study of Congress. It is therefore necessary to reflect on why the substantive issue–based research tradition was so short-lived and has yet to make a meaningful return to congressional studies. There are, I believe, central reasons for this. First, problems in measurement and specification plagued past researchers and helped bring this body of work to a halt. The tradition petered out in part because of the lack of a theoretically driven and robust coding schema that constructed "natural" categories and avoided the problems of categories that were too bulky or could not be applied across time without losing gains to historical specificity. The second reason stemmed from the strong claim, mounted most persuasively by Keith Poole and Howard Rosenthal (1997), that policy variation has little impact on the basic contours of roll call behavior. The third reason was that in the search for variations by issue content in the causal mechanisms of lawmaking, studies of legislative accomplishment did not treat specific public policies as the object of analysis but focused instead on the impact of institutions, rules, and norms on legislative outputs in general.

Every serious student of Congress knows that appropriate coding is the critical element for linking substantive policies to the behavior of members. What constitutes robust, theoretically driven, and thus appropriate coding has been controversial in past work. This is evident from an examination of the many coding classifications that have been constructed for roll votes, committee hearings, public statutes, and vetoes. Unfortunately, the main categorizations suffer from at least one of three pitfalls–over-aggregation, the absence of a motivating and orienting theoretical compass, and a dependence on time-bound policy categories. A neglected corollary issue is whether a categorization schema should be mutually exclusive, that is, whether roll votes or public statutes should be assigned a single policy code or whether it is possible to attach multiple codes to them. This issue is particularly important for public statutes with the rise of multifaceted omnibus legislation in the 1980s (see Krutz 2001).

Of attempts to classify roll calls and statutes, the most influential and dominant within congressional studies has been the five-tier policy coding created by Aage Clausen (1967, 1973). This coding schema was a feature of his search for policy domains characterized by unidimensionality and stability in the period between 1953 and 1964. Important research based on this classification demonstrated the distinct existence and effects of economic and social welfare policy dimensions in roll call voting. This research hypothesized that the former is influenced more by partisan differences and the latter by constituency constraints (Clausen and Cheney 1970), and it showed how the content of policy affected a shift from partisan to regional voting between 1933 and 1956 (Sinclair 1978). Despite these contributions, the bulk of Clausen's highly aggregated coding categories limited their utility and precision and made it difficult, and at times impossible, to specify the independent impact of important policy distinctions and differences.[3] By inserting labor votes into the category of social welfare, for example, the schema obscured the distinctiveness of roll call behavior in this policy domain (Katznelson, Geiger, and Kryder 1993; Poole and Rosenthal 1997, 111). Thus, the findings by Clausen and Cheney that lumped these issues together under this single banner were rendered suspect. Furthermore, the Clausen schema was inductively based, in that policy clustering was based on empirical research instead of theoretically generated categories.

In contrast to Clausen's schema stands the earlier work of Theodore Lowi, who began in the 1960s to publish a series of pioneering articles (1964, 1970, 1972) about discerning the determination of politics by policy. Lowi's project was vastly ambitious and inclusive—a parsimonious classification of policy areas (first characterized famously as distributive, regulatory, and redistributive) capable of defining "arenas of power" and placing a vast array of case studies across American politics in time. He hypothesized that each type of issue elicits different definitions of interest, different relations among interests, and different relations between interests and government. On this basis, he generated a deductive, predictive typology that projected outcomes from types of policy with respect to units of action (individuals, groups, associations), types of relations among units (log-rolling, coalitions, peak associations, and social classes), and structures of power (nonconflictual, pluralistic, and conflictual), as well as relative stability, loci of decision, and patterns of implementation. For Lowi, politics made policy in the most comprehensive manner, but his initiative did not move ahead quite as robustly as he had hoped. Lowi's promised research program, at least in its most programmatic and systematic incarnations, faded for reasons of coding. If Clausen's categorization suffered from too few "ordinary language" types and lumping where splitting was needed, Lowi's far more abstract schema soon proved very difficult to operationalize crisply.

There are, of course, other extant approaches to coding. However, they tend to err in the opposite direction—they often project very long inductive lists. An important example is Keith Poole's remarkable personal effort to code every roll call vote between the 1st and 100th Congresses for his joint work with Howard Rosenthal. Poole arranged the roll call votes by utilizing an extensive but unsorted inventory of policies. This approach yielded such

---

[3] Sam Peltzman (1984) has also created a specialized, highly aggregated coding scheme that focuses on budget and regulation policies.

anomalies as categories for World War I and the Korean War but none for World War II, as well as an oddly non-equivalent set of classifications that placed "Mediterranean pirates," "slavery," and "public works" on the same scale (Poole and Rosenthal 1997, 259–62).[4] The problem with such inductive lists developed in an ad hoc manner is that they have neither an implicit nor an explicit theoretical rationale and thus, when applied over time, manifest lumpiness in their categories and unevenness in analysis.

Another impressive research program that took the inductive list approach was the Policy Agendas Project of Frank Baumgartner and Bryan Jones. The design they adopted was two-tiered, marked by 19 major topics and 225 subtopics. This codification was developed inductively by first working on congressional hearings, and it was designed specifically (and, given its historically specific character, exclusively) for the post-1946 legislative environment (Baumgartner and Jones 1993; Baumgartner, Jones, and MacLeod 1998). Thus, even this impressive project replicated a rather common feature of congressional coding schemata—the restriction of substantive categorization to categories that are based on the substance of discussion, debate, and legislation at particular historical periods and consequently lack portability across the full swath of American political history.

Pioneered by Clausen, the bulk of such work in the field has focused on the post-1946 "modern Congress" and has classified roll calls and statutes legislation by period-specific categories.[5] For this reason, David Brady and Joseph Stewart's (1982) work on the policy import of realignment created two additional "time-bound" classifications appropriate, respectively, for the Civil War era and the 1890s. For each period, they replicated the method that Clausen had used to identify the small number of issue areas he found to be central in the 1950s and 1960s. Not surprisingly, their lists across periods had virtually no overlap. This approach to historicity solves the problem of transporting inapplicable categories to various time periods, but it leaves scholars dependent on controversial periodization templates (Mayhew 2002). Further, the punctuated and iterated character of the Brady-Stewart approach precludes consistent measurement of the substantive ebb and flow of legislation by policy categories because its historical character leaves out routine periods and produces an incomplete time series across policy domains.

---

[4] In addition to applying their own scheme to every roll call vote in the House and Senate between the 1st and 100th Congresses, Poole and Rosenthal (1997, 259) applied Peltzman's (1984) schema and Clausen's (1973) schema with the addition of a "miscellaneous policy" category they defined as "unclassifiable or unidentified votes; all votes concerned with the internal organization of Congress, procedural motions."

[5] Clausen (1973, 5) extended his coding to cover the years 1969 and 1970 to remove "doubt [of] the validity of projecting behavior patterns observed in the past onto the present."

Whereas all of these practitioners of substantive coding were convinced that policy variations have an independent impact on political behavior, one of the most important recent research programs has mounted a powerful case that cuts the other way. Despite Poole and Rosenthal's own inductive typology, their work has attempted to show that policy in fact does not matter, or at best belongs on the periphery of congressional studies. If a single ideological dimension defined by strong loyalty to one of two main political parties has been the central and nearly unwavering hallmark of congressional behavior regardless of policy content across the full range of American history, then it makes little sense to ask how different policy areas convene dissimilar patterns of partisanship and choice.

Poole and Rosenthal's strategy of aggregating roll calls has indeed had the effect of highlighting and discovering similarities despite differences while impeding the reverse (a point that is empirically examined in chapter 4). Their attempt to demonstrate the power of a low (usually one-dimensional) spatial model to account for roll call voting tends to obscure differences across policy domains. When they tackle specific policy issues, such as the minimum wage or interstate commerce, they tend to do so one issue at a time and outside of the ken of any approach to classification, including Poole's.

Nevertheless, Poole and Rosenthal's powerful finding has provided ammunition for the argument that studying policy substance is not a necessary component to understanding the behavior of members of Congress. Unfortunately, conflating their findings over the low dimensionality of the political space with the idea that members do not have different preferences across issue areas is simply not correct. Regardless, their findings greatly reduced the energy in the Congress subfield for studying policy substance.[6] This book attempts to reverse this trend, partially by showing that members can have distinct preferences even in highly unidimensional Congresses (a point discussed in detail in chapter 4).

Much the same case can be made for studies of policy as a dependent variable. Despite the tradition of congressional research that places policy at the center of explanations of the impact of behavior and institutions on policy outputs, the explicit study of legislative outputs has not developed nearly as fast as research that focuses on the role of institutions and environmental factors as influences on legislative behavior. There is now a considerable store

---

[6]Poole and Rosenthal (1997, 27) find that a single dimension can account for approximately 80 percent of the individual decisions (roll calls) of members of Congress, and that a two-dimensional model accounts for nearly 85 percent of these decisions. In other words, most of the decisions of members of Congress are captured by a common (ideological) dimension. This, of course, means that 15 to 20 percent of the decisions are captured by higher dimensions and need explanation. Also, very little work has assessed how issues leave the first dimension and enter the second or higher dimensions.

of knowledge on the influence of the quest for reelection on how legislators design internal institutions and the impact of factors such as constituency and party pressures on the roll call voting behavior of members of Congress. The imbalance between what is known about individual member behavior and what is known about the determinants of actual legislative accomplishment has not gone unnoticed. Indeed, a call for greater balance through the explicit study of policy as a dependent variable was made in an underappreciated review essay written two decades ago by David Brady and Joseph Cooper (1981). They argued that to better understand and pinpoint the effects of institutional changes on the policy process, Congress must also be studied as an independent variable, with the output side of the equation including surges and slumps in important legislation. Cooper and Brady's call for macro-level analysis did not include a specific call for studying policy substance. Nonetheless, there is no reason to assume a priori that legislative outcomes are consistent across this expanse. In fact, theoretical work within the Congress subfield leads us to expect differences across policy types.

In summary, the substantive tradition in political science has been greatly diminished primarily because of a combination of the shortcomings of previous coding schemas and misinterpretation of the highly influential findings of Poole and Rosenthal to suggest incorrectly that policy substance does not matter. The next section shows how literatures in the Congress subfield and APD can be leveraged to develop an appropriate coding schema that will reinvigorate the study of policy issue substance.

INTRODUCING A NEW POLICY CLASSIFICATION SCHEMA

Congressional studies, policy studies, and APD have all omitted the systematic study of policy issue substance from their research agendas. This section introduces the first necessary tool for bringing policy issue substance front and center in the study of American politics—a policy coding schema that transcends subfields yet accommodates scholars working on diverse topics.

When policy is thought of as an independent variable, scholars, assuming that legislators hold distinctive preferences about different types of policies, treat preferences as keenly affected by the substance of policy issues. When one is interested in explaining what government does, policy serves as the dependent variable. The coding schema developed here is an instrument to parse and organize both situations. Previous schemata have been devised, often with the goal of coding one but not both types of data. Research that attempts to determine the role of policy in the study of Congress in each regard cannot be accomplished without being able to parse policy into meaningful discrete categories. Developing a schema that is able to code roll calls and lawmaking is not an easy task, especially given that roll calls are often procedural, sometimes not related to policymaking, and often more oriented toward taking a position than lawmaking.

No taxonomy is innocent. Acts of classification, even when they seem unguided or purely inductive, are at once theoretical statements about how the world might fruitfully be studied within the ambit of a particular perspective on social reality and empirical claims about how the world actually is organized. I developed the coding schema described here with the understanding that good categorization requires both motivating principles and a high degree of recognition by those who share in the experience being cataloged. I also considered series of practical, instrumental ways to make the schema both useful and reliable.

Measurement cannot be divorced from theory. In constructing this schema, I found the necessary scholarly support in theoretical work primarily from the Congress and American political development subfields. Three central ideas from APD underlie this classification of policy. As a representative democracy, the United States enacts public policies that define its character as a state. Although its legislature may be sui generis, its assertions of sovereignty over people and territory, its ensemble of institutions and rules of governance, the patterns of its transactions with other states in a world of states, and the terms of its exchanges with its citizens and the economy are all hallmarks of "stateness" that the United States shares with other countries. The first goal, then, has been to construct a way of organizing policy that makes it possible to understand the particularities of state formation in the United States in comparative perspective. This has been a core goal of APD since the publication of Stephen Skowronek's *Building a New American State* (1982), but as already noted, it has been only rarely pursued in this research tradition by way of systematic studies of congressional agendas and policy choices.

The United States, moreover, is not just a state but, given the centrality of representation to its constitutional design, arguably the world's most liberal state. Rather than take this feature of its character as fixed or given, the schema has been designed to make it possible to probe the contours, limits, and contested content of this liberalism, with no a priori assumptions about its special place in the realm of ideas or ideology. Rather, liberalism is conceptualized, first, as an open doctrine based on a small number of core values—including government by consent, political representation, toleration, and irreducible rights for its citizens—that can bond, as it has, with a wide variety of other clusters of ideas, be they republican, democratic, authoritarian, racist, populist, religious, or socialist. Second, liberalism is conceptualized as organized and regulated relationships linking the state to other states, to the economy, and to citizens in civil society. Both aspects are contested and changeable; both pivot on configurations of public policy. By focusing on Congress and policy, we are able to chronicle these contests and assign them empirical content at particular moments and across wider expanses of historical time.

Providing a new way of studying American political history thus constitutes the third core goal of this approach. Social scientists do not lack ways to parse the past. Historians and political scientists have access to a variety of descriptive and analytic periodizations, ranging from presidential labels ("the Age of Jackson") to atmospheric tags ("the Gilded Age") to sets of animating movements ("the Progressive era") to long swaths of time before and after key events ("antebellum") to scientific claims about temporality ("realignment"). Hoping to contribute tools for fresh approaches to the fundamental task of periodization, I have designed an approach to policy coding that, although not time-bound, is sensitive to variations in the content of policy at different historical moments. By making a detailed mapping of the policy landscape of the United States possible over time, this schema should help us better understand such temporal concepts as critical junctures, path dependence, and the import of sequencing.

Thoughtful coding, in combining a focus on representation and public policy, can advance understanding of American state formation, the status of liberalism, and the character of temporality in the American experience. If these goals are to be secured, it is best to break with the convention that forces policy substance into a single level of aggregation and to refuse the choice between deductive and inductive approaches. As research questions shift, so do appropriate constellations of policy and strategies of inquiry. More specifically, it is important that scholars be able to classify either by coding at a very particular level and moving up a ladder when they combining these particulars, or by starting with large categories and moving down a ladder toward more particularity and historical specificity. For these reasons, this schema appears in tiers. The first tier, with only four categories, seeks to capture the basic features of state policy found in all modern states and adjudicated by legislatures in all representative democracies. The third tier, with seventy categories, is intended to be an inclusive set of "experience-near" classifications at a comparable level of analysis that contain the full range of policies in American history. Between these two is a fourteen-category middle tier that acts as a hinge connecting the deductive and analytical first tier with the inductive and descriptive third. This second tier is both a specification of the theory beneath the coding at the first level and a more summative statement of policy activity than the third. Here, the focus on state formation, liberalism, and historicity is joined to an inclusive and logically consistent set of policy categories in a fine grain.

Guided by the work of historians, political theorists, and scholars of American political development, I have created categories that are appropriate to the workings of a representative democracy in building a modern national state and creating public policies across time. Resolutely institutional and substantive, this approach centers on what the national state is, what it does, and how it structures key sets of linkages that define the character of its regime.

Such an approach gives rise to another objective, one having to do with the character of political science and the place of American political studies within it. The schema is designed to organize an approach to policy coding that will be of interest and use more generally beyond the confines of congressional studies or American politics. Colleagues who work in comparative politics, political theory, and international relations should be able to integrate their questions and categories into this approach. For this reason, as one example, the schema does not limit itself in the first tier to the familiar dualism of domestic and international affairs, which effectively lumps everything that does not qualify as international into the domestic category. Among its other deficits, this dualism leaves out consideration of policies that clearly overlap these arenas, such as those concerned with membership and boundaries.

Although I explicitly designed the schema to probe many questions within American political development, I also went to great lengths to make it suitable to empirically evaluate important theoretical work within the Congress sub-field. For example, the Congress literature suggests that members of Congress have different incentives when legislation deals with public goods (nondivisible goods such as national defense) versus particularistic (private) goods whose benefits accrue to a limited number of constituents. This theoretical work—for example, the work on particularistic good provision (Ferejohn 1974; Wilson 1986)—often appeals to uncertainty about membership in a winning coalition (see, for example, Weingast 1979) or uncertainty about belonging, given claims about political parties having originated to coordinate members' expectations and resolve uncertainty (see, for example, Aldrich 1995). To test such propositions, a coding schema must be able to separate such policies (laws) or positions (roll calls). The schema presented in table 2.1 was designed to do just that.

The first tier of the schema designates four basic elements common to modern states and reserves "domestic affairs" to a specific policy zone that encompasses substantive policy outputs but is distinct from the zone of policies that define the characteristics of sovereignty or the organization and scope of the state as an institution. The first tier also includes four categories that are specific to the United States and Congress.

Within tier 1, the fitting first category is sovereignty, the defining characteristic of states, from those fashioned after feudalism in early modern Europe to the current members of the United Nations. Most scholars of American politics outside of the field of American political development pay little, if any, attention to the issue of sovereignty. Instead, issues of sovereignty are often treated as domestic politics by scholars of Congress and public policy. I believe that sovereignty policy is distinct from domestic affairs and deserves its own zone. As a starting point, sovereignty policy refers to the state's indivisible claim to rule legitimately over particular people and places. Hence it is concerned with the very existence, boundaries, and membership

Table 2.1 A Three–Tiered Coding Schema

Tier 1	Tier 2	Tier 3
Sovereignty	Liberty	Loyalty and expression; religion; privacy
	Membership and nation	Commemoration and national culture; Immigration and naturalization
	Civil rights	African Americans; American Indians; women; other minority groups; voting rights
	Boundaries	Frontier settlement; Indian removal and compensation; state admission/union composition; territories and colonies
Organization and scope	Government organization	Congressional organization, administration, and personnel; executive organization administration, and personnel; judicial organization, administration, and personnel; impeachment/misconduct
	Representation	Census/apportionment; elections; groups and interests
	Constitutional amendments	Federalism and terms of office; political participation and rights; other
International relations	Defense	Air force organization and deployment; army organization and deployment; naval organization and deployment; defense organization (general); militias; military installations; civil/homeland defense
	Geopolitics	Diplomacy and intelligence; foreign aid; international organizations aid; international organizations
	International political economy	Maritime; trade and tariffs; economic international organizations

Table 2.1 Continued.

Tier 1	Tier 2	Tier 3
Domestic affairs	Agriculture and food	Agricultural technology; farmers and farming support; fishing and livestock
	Planning and resources	Corporatism; environment; infrastructure and public works; national resources; social knowledge; post office; transportation; wage and price controls; interstate compacts and federalism; urban, and rural and regional development
	Political economy	Appropriations; multiple-agency; business and capital markets; fiscal/taxation; labor markets and unions; monetary; regulation/economic
	Social policy	Children and youth; crime; disaster; education; handicapped and disabilities; civilian health; housing; military pensions/benefits and civilian compensation; public works and volunteer employment; social regulation; social insurance; transfers/poverty
District of Columbia		
Housekeeping		
Quasi–Private		
Public/Quasi–Private		

Notes: Tier 3 categories are separated by semicolons.

of the national regime. The concept of sovereignty is of central importance in comparative politics and APD, in large part because it is concerned with two issues intrinsic to the modern state: territoriality and citizenship. As noted by T. Alexander Aleinikoff (2002, 11), "A national state confronts issues of sovereignty when it determines its borders, its members, and its powers," and the American state is no exception. Territoriality—authority over a defined geographical area and the ability to regulate its boundaries—has long been recognized as a crucial element of the sovereign state: "It is the part of the Nation, or of its sovereign, to enforce justice throughout the territory subject to it" (Vattel 1916, 139). Scholars in APD are paying increasing attention to the issue of territoriality as they begin to assess the causes and consequences of American expansion (Levinson and Sparrow 2005).

Citizenship is likewise a core component of sovereignty, since it is the central mechanism—along with its corollary, alienage—by which a population is linked to the modern state, membership is delineated, and a collective civic identity is constituted (Bosniak 2006). T. H. Marshall (1950, 18) defined citizenship as "a status bestowed on those who are full members of a community" where "all who possess the status are equal with respect to the rights and duties with which the status is endowed." Political contestation over securing or abridging the equality of rights for legally recognized citizens, as well as over the inclusion of different peoples and groups within the category of citizen, has been a central feature of the historical development of citizenship. Accordingly, citizenship laws "are among the most fundamental of political creations" (Smith 1997, 31). Although much attention has been given to the construction of citizenship by the judiciary, the role of Congress in establishing the boundaries of membership and the gradations of status is critical to understanding the development of citizenship in the United States. It has been a core concept in APD, notably in works concerning the exclusion of African Americans (King 1995; Valelly 2004), women (Mettler 1998; Ritter 2000), and immigrants (Bosniak 2006; Ngai 2004) and the importance of liberalism in shaping American understandings of national identity and politics (Smith 1997). Immigration and naturalization policy lies at the intersection of territory and citizenship and has been long seen as a core dimension of sovereignty. Immigration policy and the public arguments surrounding it have shaped the American nation and the ways in which sovereignty is understood there (Shanks 2001; Tichenor 2002). In short, sovereignty policy concerns policies that are crucial in the construction of the governing authority of the modern state (Orren and Skowronek 2004, 123–26). Governing authority does not rest solely on coercive power or the construction of an infrastructure of state capacity, the focus of much of the formative literature in APD (Bensel 1990; Skowronek 1982). The modern state is equally reliant on various forms of legitimacy, including the construction and affirmation of the population as a distinct people (Smith 2003).[7]

---

[7]This was noted by Harold Laski (1917, 12), who argued that the "true meaning of sovereignty [is] not in the coercive power possessed by its instrument, but in the fused goodwill for which it stands."

Sovereignty

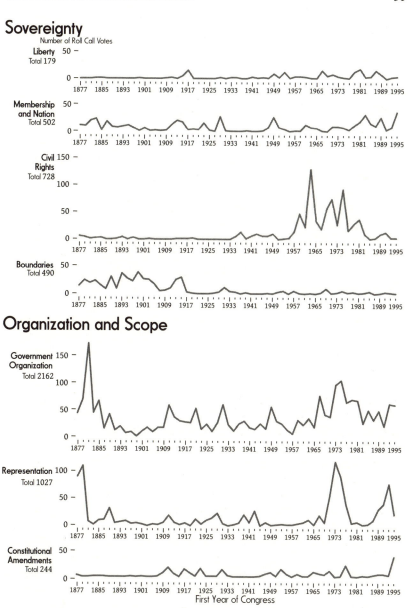

Number of Roll Call Votes

Figure 2.1
Senate Roll Call Votes, 1877 to 1996

International Affairs

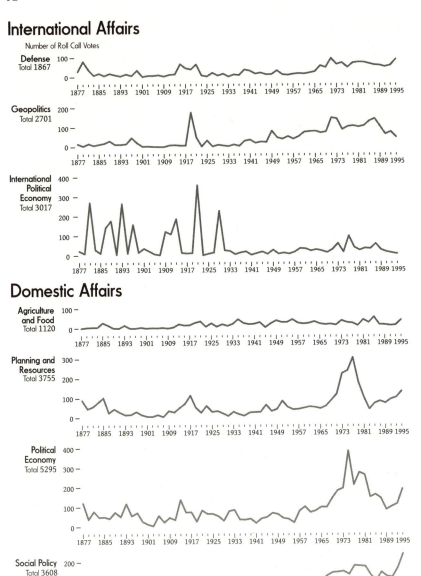

Domestic Affairs

Figure 2.1
Continued.

Miscellaneous

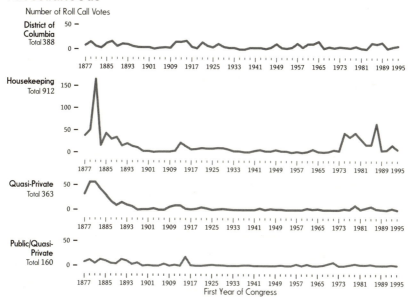

Figure 2.1
Continued.

The second category, organization and scope, concerns the substantive reach and range of activities and the institutional elaboration of the national government and its instruments for governing, including its basic constitutional rules, norms, formal organization, and terms of political participation. This, too, is a category of policies not ordinarily separated out in this way. Identifying policy that is specifically related to the institutions that constitute the policymaking apparatus opens the possibility of systematically measuring when and why institutions change. Although not limited to the organization of Congress, this category helps advance research that focuses on how this institution organizes itself while drawing on other categories to trace links between how Congress sets its own rules and what it produces as policy outputs. Policymaking takes place within a separation-of-powers system in the United States, so this category also allows us to track formal rule changes that relate to the office of the president and the judiciary (Cameron, Lapinski and Riemann 2000; Cameron 2000). By focusing on the character and institutional composition and rules of government, the first two categories taken together make it possible to develop systematic measures that place congressional decision-making at the center of the historical development of the national state without reducing "state-making," as some literatures do, to a single

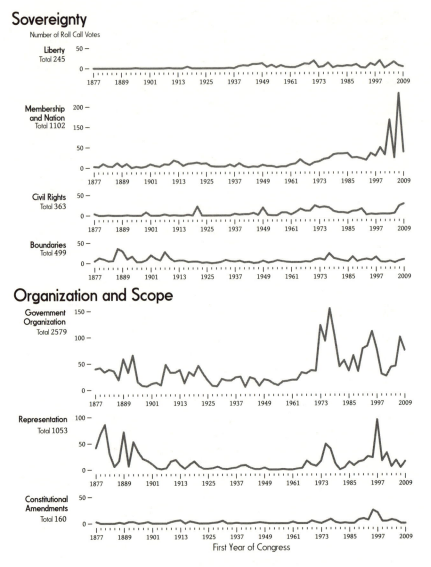

Figure 2.2
House Roll Call Votes, 1877 to 2010

continuum that runs from weak to strong, where "strong" too simply connotes a capable executive.

The two remaining main categories in the first tier of coding concern the outputs of government. International relations refers to the geopolitical and

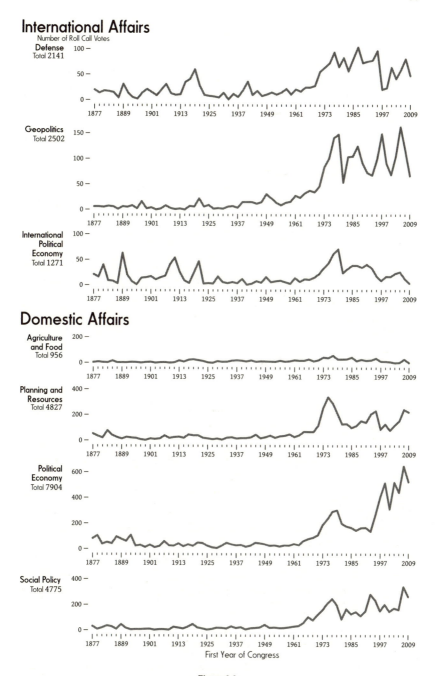

Figure 2.2
Continued.

Miscellaneous

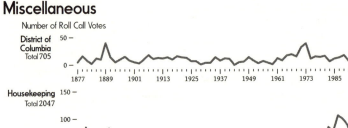

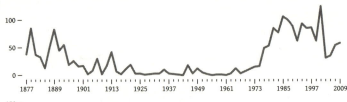

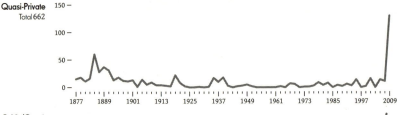

Figure 2.2
Continued.

economic transactions between the United States as a unit in the global system of states and other sovereign states (as well as the international system and its formal and informal organizations). Tier 2 for the international relations category is divided into defense, geopolitics, and international political economy. These divisions reflect the separation of existing international relations into separate areas of research: security studies, international organizations, and international political economy. Though there have been major works that attempted to bridge the divide between these separate areas of research, for the most part research continues separately, with specific journals dedicated to each topic in the subfield of international relations.[8] In addition, in their 2008

---

[8]For instance, a major point of contention for many in international relations is the extent to which matters of security and political economy can be combined, and if so, how. For a description of the evolution of these divisions within the subfield, see Katzenstein, Keohane, and Krasner (1998), Strange (1970), Baldwin (1995) and Nye and Lynn-Jones (1988).

Sovereignty

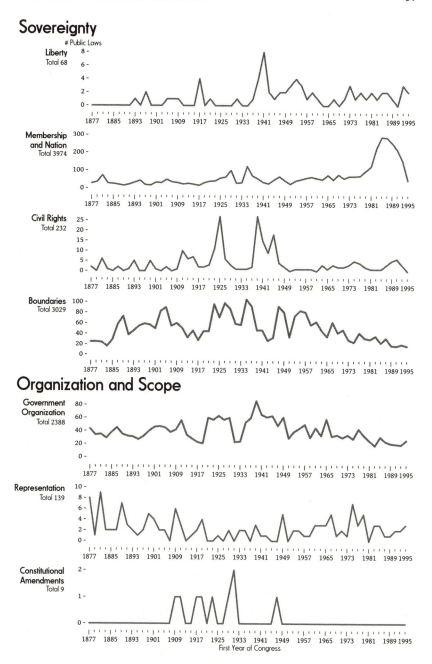

Figure 2.3
Public Laws by Tier 2 Categories, 1877 to 1996

International Affairs

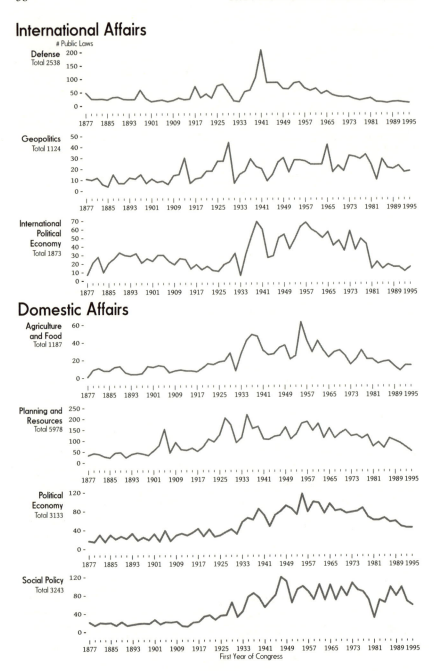

Figure 2.3
Continued.

Miscellaneous

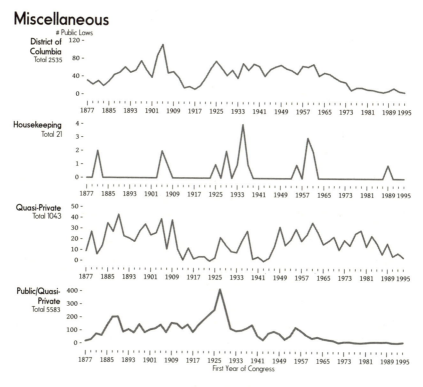

Figure 2.3
Continued.

survey of international relations scholars, Richard Jordan and his colleagues (2009) show that the biggest divisions within the subfield of international relations occur between these three areas.[9]

Domestic affairs is the category that covers the public policies that shape the ties between government and the economy and between government and the welfare of its citizens. As described earlier, domestic affairs is different from many other coding schemas in that issues dealing with sovereignty, organization and scope, and defense are omitted from this category.

Besides the four main tier 1 categories, I found it necessary to create four additional tier 1 categories. The first of these, a District of Columbia category, recognizes that Congress has served, in effect, as the legislature for the District

---

[9]Their survey results show that international relations scholars in the United States identify their field of study as "international security" (22 percent), "international political economy" (14 percent), and "international organizations" (6 percent).

of Columbia. The second tier 1 category, housekeeping, is designed for roll calls on procedural matters, including most printing matters. This category illustrates important differences between the coding of public statutes and roll calls. The last two tier 1 categories deal with Congress and particularistic goods. The first of these, labeled quasi-private, deals with bills that address economic benefits to particular individuals and single-named companies, firms, or organizations. No omnibus bill, therefore, can fall into this category, unless amendments to an omnibus bill are made for specific claimants. The second of these last two categories, public/quasi-private, deals with bills that involve specific benefits that are not for individuals or single-named companies but include the features of a public good, including construction of a specific bridge or building, administration of individual public buildings, and transfers of public property, such as a tract of land, a building, or an office, to a city or county.

Thus, the four main categories of the first tier of coding are tied to what modern sovereign states are and do across time. By keeping these large categories constant, it is possible to see the relative emphasis of lawmaking in distinct periods and probe whether policy coalitions vary from one domain to another.

Because these four categories are bulky, the second tier divides each first tier into three or four "blueprint" subcategories. That is, for each class of policies in the first tier, the second tier identifies the layered elements that together compose its constellation. Thus, sovereignty in a representative democracy always entails decisions about liberty, membership and the demographic composition of the nation, civil rights, and physical boundaries. Organization and scope in such a regime is composed of decisions about constitutional structure, governmental organization, and rules of political representation. International relations divides into the triad of defense, geopolitics, and international political economy, whereas domestic affairs, ever since the out-set of the Republic, have divided into policy judgments about agriculture and food, planning and resources, political economy, and social policy. By elaborating this second tier of issues to be found at every time period, it becomes possible not only to assess the consistency and diversity of ide-ologies and coalitions within and across tier 1 categories at any specific temporal moment but also to pick up the dynamics of change across periods. Figures 2.1, 2.2, and 2.3 provide an aggregate breakdown for all House and Senate roll calls and all public statutes (laws), including the breakdown for specific historical periods. The figures provide information on both tier 1 and tier 2 categories.

These distinctions are still not fine-grained enough to surmount the prob-lems of aggregation observed in other coding schemata. Utilizing a detailed review of congressional committee responsibilities, budget categories, and classifications of existing coding approaches, each second-tier category is subdivided into two to thirteen tier 3 substantive classifications intended to be mutually exclusive and comprehensive.[10] Over time, the relative weight of these sites of policy changes significantly. The appendix to this chapter provides a detailed description of the coding rules and examples of how policies are placed in particular categories.

CONCLUSION

In sum, the classification is designed to code congressional roll calls and public statutes by policy area guided by visible criteria for the assemblage of categories, combining a strongly deductive, institutionally and state-oriented approach to the first two tiers with a more inductive approach to filling out the third. The approach is detailed enough to discriminate between clusters of policy and avoid problems of over-aggregation and yet not so lengthy as to cease to be based on clear categorizations. The coding schema provides policy classifications that can be applied and combined at different levels of aggregation, thus avoiding the pitfalls of approaches that are either too broad or too detailed and unwieldy.

APPENDIX: CODING SCHEMA

A. *Sovereignty* is the central feature of modern stateness; that is, it is the defining characteristic of states fashioned after feudalism in early modern Europe to the present. Though a rich and contested term, it refers to the state's indivisible claim to rule legitimately over particular populations and territories. Hence it is concerned with the very existence, boundaries, and membership of the national regime.

   1. *Liberty* covers legislation defining the scope of citizens' civil liberty

      (a) *Loyalty and expression* includes subversion or protection from subversion (espionage, antigovernment propaganda,

---

[10] A potential problem for the coding scheme arises from the surge in omnibus bills in the U.S. Congress. Although omnibus legislation dates back at least to the 1940s, there was a tremendous rise of such legislation in the 1980s (for a detailed history of omnibus bills, see Krutz 2001). All appropriation bills receive a double tier 3 coding because each is coded as both appropriation and substantive policy. If an appropriation bill is omnibus, its second tier 3 coding is "omnibus." Omnibus bills are not limited to appropriations. Consequently, all omnibus legislation is identified as such, but when possible I tried to determine the primary policy content of each bill and give it a substantive policy coding. Technically, this maneuver violates the mutually exclusive coding rule.

restrictions on travel during wartime, imputed loyalty to other governments, and movements such as fascism and communism

(b) *Religion* includes the separation and the relationship between church and state.

(c) *Privacy* includes consumer privacy, as well as the protection of worker records, employee drug and polygraph testing, and government and police wiretapping. The protection of medical records would fall in this subcategory. Also included is privacy as it relates to the Internet and computer technology.

2. *Membership and Nation* covers rules for entering, in part or in full, the communities of citizens and political participants and for marking the character of the nation.

(a) *Commemorations and national culture* includes holidays, memorials, and other means to officially recall people and events, plus depositories of cultural heritage, such as the National Archive and the Smithsonian Institution, and programs geared to advance a national culture.

(b) *Immigration and naturalization* includes entry and exit. Family reunification and deportation fall in this subcategory except when motivated by "liberty" issues. Also included are rules for citizenship, procedures for becoming a naturalized citizen such as literacy tests for immigrants, and rules for dealing with refugees and their legal status, except when this involves direct negotiations with a foreign country. Legislation on agencies that deal with immigration issues in part or in whole fall in this subcategory.

3. *Civil rights* covers laws and roll calls on the inclusion, exclusion, or protection of racialized minorities, especially African Americans.

(a) *The African Americans* subcategory includes slavery and slave trade taxation, relevant Reconstruction legislation (such as antilynching bills), segregation and desegregation of public accommodations, antidiscrimination legislation (as in employment and housing), busing, and affirmative action. It does not include roll calls on voting rights.

(b) *The Native Americans* subcategory covers the regulation of conduct, protection, political autonomy, and cultural rights. It also includes legislation concerning Indian reservations (such as rights to hunt and fish and general uses of territory), as well as diplomatic and economic interactions with Native American tribes.

(c) *Other minority groups* includes the protection of specifically defined minority groups other than African Americans or Native Americans—for example, the protection of Chinese persons and antidiscrimination with respect to homosexuality, age, disease, and disability (such as employment discrimination against the handicapped).

(d) *Women* includes legislation and regulation against gender discrimination, as in employment, salary, and university sports programs. This subcategory does not include voting rights, such as women's suffrage.

(e) *Voting rights* includes the franchise, its exercise, and its restriction (as in poll taxes).

4. *Boundaries* is concerned with the spatial dimensions and location of the American "frontier" and the extension of national sovereignty to particular geographic areas, excluding war and diplomacy between the United States and other recognized sovereign states. It also includes issues dealing with the stability of the union.

(a) *Frontier settlement* includes various aspects of westward push, including homestead acts.

(b) *Indian removal and compensation* includes treaties, payments, and military operations to remove Indians to new locations as well as payments to Indian tribes.

(c) *State admission/union composition* includes roll calls or public statutes to consider moving specific territories to the status of states and also votes that involve the stability of the union.

(d) *Territories and colonies* includes the definition and governance of land under U.S. sovereignty or possession before admission to the status of a state (for example incorporation of private companies). The annexation of territory (for example, Texas and Hawaii) falls in this subcategory.

B. *Organization and scope* is concerned with the substantive reach and range of activities and the institutional elaboration of the state and its governing instruments, including its basic rules, norms, formal organization, and terms of participation.

1. *Government organization* covers laws and votes on the structure, scale, and rules of the national government.

   (a) *Congressional organization, administration, and personnel* includes all internal rules of Congress, including the salaries of members of the House and Senate.

   (b) *Executive organization, administration, and personnel* includes the organization of the executive branch as a whole as defined by reorganization bills, shifts in cabinet scale and responsibilities, the creation of cabinet-level departments, and the means available to Congress to monitor the executive branch, including requests for public-sector pensions and promotion in the federal service; appointments to federal positions and the preparation and maintenance of government records fall in this subcategory. It also includes issues concerning public access to information, as in the Freedom of Information Act. It does not include the creation of commissions or boards, which fall under their substantive policy areas.

   (c) *Impeachment/misconduct* covers impeachment trials and misconduct trials dealing with public officials in the legislative, judicial, and executive branches.

   (d) *Judicial organization, administration, and personnel* includes the organization of the federal court system and programs of access like the Legal Services Corporation.

2. *Representation* covers the terms of participation by individual and group members of civil society.

    (a) *Census/apportionment* includes census legislation and adjustments to the number of seats held by states after a given census.

    (b) *Elections* includes contested elections and rules for elections and participation, such as the Hatch Act, soldier voting bills, and campaign finance.

    (c) *Groups and interests* includes rules for lobbying, registration, governance, and access by pressure groups.

3. *Constitutional amendments* are attempted additions to the Constitution.

    (a) *Federalism and terms of office* includes relevant constitutional amendments.

    (b) *Political participation and rights* includes relevant constitutional amendments.

    (c) *Other* includes all other constitutional amendments.

C. *International relations* concerns geopolitical and economic transactions between the United States as a unit in the global system of states and other sovereign states (as well as the international system and its formal and informal organizations).

1. *Defense* covers the structure, scale, and rules of the national government.

    (a) *Air force organization and deployment* includes decisions about air force structure, weapons, and personnel.

    (b) *Army organization and deployment* includes decisions about the army's structure, weapons, and personnel.

    (c) *Conscription/enlistment* includes the mobilization of human power.

    (d) *Militias* includes state and local military forces.

(e) *Naval organization and deployment* includes decisions about the navy's and marines' structure, weapons, and personnel. It also includes the protection of commerce on the high seas prior to the establishment of a formal navy.

(f) *Defense organization* includes decisions about the structure, weapons, and personnel of the armed forces as a whole or more than one branch, including the powers of the president as commander in chief.

(g) *Civil/homeland defense* covers activities to guard the territory and population within the United States from military invasion, bombing, and terrorist assaults, including the use of biological weapons against civilians. Examples include civil defense facilities, the emergency broadcasting system, anti-anthrax efforts, and airport screening when related to homeland threats.

2. *Geopolitics* includes the extension and management of American power and security in a global setting.

(a) *Diplomacy/intelligence* covers negotiations and relations with other states in peace and in war, including treaties, policy pronouncements, interstate claims for compensation, and declarations of war, as well as the collection and dissemination of information on foreign countries (for example, the CIA). This subcategory also includes trade policy that is geared toward geopolitical ends rather than economic ends, such as trade sanctions against Iraq or Cuba. It also includes policy aimed at protecting Americans living abroad.

(b) *Foreign aid* includes non-military and military transfers by grant and loan to other countries, as in lend-lease, reparations, and the Marshall Plan and programs of development assistance such as the Peace Corps.

(c) *International organizations* includes formal organizations that are more than bilateral institutions, such as the League of Nations and the United Nations, international tribunals, including those for war crimes, and NGOs (nongovernmental organizations) like the International Red Cross.

3. *International political economy* includes the global extension and management of the American economy.

   (a) *Maritime* covers shipping, the merchant marines, and trade routes, including the Panama Canal.

   (b) *Trade/tariffs* includes taxes on and regulation of imports and exports, negotiations with other countries over rates, ports of entry, and free trade zones, customhouses, and international trade regimes and organizations concerned with trade, such as GATT (the General Agreement on Tariffs and Trade) and NAFTA (North American Free Trade Agreement).

   (c) *Economic international organizations* includes formal organizations such as the World Bank and the IMF (International Monetary Fund). Institutions such as the Bretton Woods agreement fall in this subcategory.

D. *Domestic affairs* is concerned with public policies shaping both the ties between government and the economy and between the government and the welfare of its citizens.

   1. *Agriculture and food* includes farming and its conditions.

      (a) *Agricultural technology* includes technical assistance geared to better crop production, including soil conservation, seed innovations, the diffusion of technical information to farmers, statistical studies, and the creation of educational institutions designated primarily to advance agriculture.

      (b) *Farmers/farming support* includes disaster relief, guarantees to loan categories, assistance to farmers, including legislation subsidizing both productions of commodities and decisions not to plant and produce, and programs under the authority of the Commodity Credit Corporation that are not commodity subsidies as such. It also includes reductions of aid to farmers, as well as appropriations for the Department of Agriculture and agriculture programs.

      (c) *Fishing and livestock* includes subsidies and aid with respect to non-plant agricultural production.

2. *Planning and resources* includes authoritative and negotiated non-market emplacement and allocation of public goods, private capital, and labor.

   (a) *Corporatism* includes negotiated agreements about production and consumption between representatives of business, labor and government and shifts to the locus of production between the private and public sectors. It also includes NIRA (National Industrial Recovery Act).

   (b) *Environment* includes legislation concerned with the quality of the air, water and land, and the protection of nature, animate and inanimate, and the disposal of waste, including nuclear waste.

   (c) *Infrastructure/public works* includes all non-transportation-related initiatives, including communications infrastructure, dams, flood prevention, harbors, the TVA (Tennessee Valley Authority), and electrification.

   (d) *National resources* includes reclamation projects, land affairs (whether civilian or sale of military land), minerals, energy (but not construction of infrastructure), forests and forest fires, national parks, production plants brought under public ownership or returned to private ownership, and the sale of government surplus goods. Land affairs dealt with here exclude those concerned with frontier settlement.

   (e) *Social knowledge* includes systematic government-funded efforts to enhance the production of social and scientific knowledge, including federal planning agencies concerned with resources and the investigation of resources, government funding of programs that involve science and research—such as NSF (National Science Foundation), NIH (National Institutes of Health), NIMH (National Institute of Mental Health), scientific expeditions and surveys in the nineteenth century, and space programs—and public broadcasting.

   (f) *Post office* includes all postal affairs, excluding the civil service.

(g) *Transportation* includes road and rail transit, canals, lighthouses, mass transit, air travel, and airports.

(h) *Wage and price controls* includes non-market interventions setting levels for wages and prices by governmental authority; it also includes rationing.

(i) *Interstate compacts/federalism* includes arrangements between the states brokered by the federal government. These include boundary questions, rivers, and other national resources. It also includes interstate relations such as financial transfers (excluding repayment of loans to states, which would be under monetary policy), revenue-sharing measures, and interactions between the federal government and one or several states.

(j) *Urban, rural, and regional development* includes programs aimed at promoting economic growth and development in specific locations such as cities and regions, excluding policies that fit specifically in a substantive category under *Planning and resources*, which are then coded by the more specific policy (for example, mass transit or public works projects).

3. *Political economy* includes legislation shaping rules and conditions within which the economy and the economic choices of individuals and collectivities operate.

(a) *Appropriations* includes all appropriation bills, including making appropriations and temporal extensions of appropriations.

(b) *Business/capital markets* includes aid to firms, government relations with firms and government purchasing from firms, antitrust across sectors and industries (general legislation), torts, the military-industrial complex, and information and statistical reports (for example, Department of Commerce statistical studies). It also includes banking-related legislation but not the Federal Reserve, bankruptcies (general not firm-specific), the RFC (Reconstruction Finance Corporation), the regulation of securities, and other agencies and activities that shape and regulate the operation of capital markets.

(c) *Fiscal/taxation* covers budgets, including debt ceilings, revenue bills, and legislation within the boundaries of the United States aimed at determining fiscal aggregates relevant to macroeconomic performance, and the fiscal duties of the Treasury such as the collection, safe-keeping, and deposit of the revenue.

(d) *Labor markets/unions* includes rules and information (such as statistical studies of the Department of Labor) for shaping and regulating conditions of employment such as wages, hours, and health and safety. This subcategory also includes legislation setting the terms and conditions for the existence and growth of trade unions.

(e) *Monetary* includes Federal Reserve and Treasury functions related to monetary policy, including gold and silver standards, the value of the dollar, bond sales (including war bonds), legislation to repay and refund the public debt, and monetary aggregates.

(f) *Economic regulation* includes all economic regulatory activities through independent regulatory commissions (such as the Interstate Commerce Commission [ICC], the Federal Communications Commission [FCC], and the Federal Aviation Administration [FAA]) of sectors and industries, as well as patents, copyrights, and trademarks, but excluding the regulation of capital and labor markets, unions, and the environment.

4. *Social policy* covers the well-being or welfare (economic and social) of the population.

(a) *Children/youth* includes policy targeted at children and youth, except overlapping transfer programs such as WIC (Women, Infants, and Children programs). Child care, parental leave, and school lunch programs fall in this subcategory.

(b) *Crime* includes legislation dealing with police, organized crime, surveillance, and narcotics. Issues such as sentencing, definitions of crimes, the death penalty, statutes of limitation, and jurisdiction are also included in this subcategory.

(c) *Disaster* includes all relief efforts resulting from natural disaster (flooding, hurricane, cyclone, and so on).

(d) *Education* includes all school-related federal policy, except certain nutrition programs such as subsidized lunches.

(e) *Handicapped/disabilities* includes legislation aimed at improving the quality of life of the handicapped. Policies aimed at the deaf and blind, along with other disabilities, in this subcategory. It also includes policy aimed at making buildings and transportation service handicapped-accessible.

(f) *Health (civilian)* includes legislation dealing with the physical and mental health of the nation. This includes the regulation of prescription drugs, medical devices, and medical procedures and the regulation of food and projects for health reasons. Disease control, inoculation, mandatory health insurance, and family leave are included. Military-related health measures are excluded. Programs dealing with the physical and mental well-being of the elderly fall in this subcategory.

(g) *Housing* includes public housing, housing for the elderly, home mortgages, and other related measures.

(h) *Military pensions/benefits and civilian compensation* (including military pensions but not social security) includes pensions, war-related compensation, land grants, veterans' housing, health benefits (VA hospital privileges), job training, and college-related benefits (GI Bill). Includes compensation to civilians over war- or conflict-related claims (such as property impounded because of an embargo).

(i) *Public works and volunteer employment* includes national government employment-related programs and volunteer employment, such as the WPA (Works Progress Administration), VISTA (Volunteers in Service to America), and Americorps.

(j) *Social regulation* includes the regulation of social behavior and conduct, such as enforcement of Prohibition, and issues of sexual preference and reproduction, including abortion. (Note that abortion falls in this subcategory because legislation is concerned mostly with appropriations to clinics, not with the legality of abortion.) It also includes regulations, such as seat belt laws, to decrease health risk and the regulation of firearms.

(k) *Social insurance* deals with policies that protect and secure against the hazards of the labor market as a whole and with respect to particular industries, including unemployment insurance, social security, and workers' compensation and industry-specific social insurance such as the Railroad Retirement Act. Specific policies such as ADC (Aid to Dependent Children) that were included in the original Social Security Act would initially be coded under *social insurance* but subsequently would be included within *transfers.*

(l) *Poverty transfers* includes direct cash assistance for relief such as FERA (Federal Emergency Relief Administration), AFDC (Aid to Families with Dependent Children), and in-kind programs such as food stamps. It also includes omnibus poverty programs such as the establishment of the OEO (Office of Economic Opportunity).

E. *District of Columbia* bills are treated as a distinctive category; Congress has served, in effect, as the legislature for Washington, DC. As a result, there are a good many roll calls in this category.

F. *Housekeeping* roll calls are concerned with procedural matters, including most printing matters. Note that the ICPSR codes cannot be used to conclude that we are dealing with a procedural bill. For example, when motions for adjournment, which ordinarily would be considered *housekeeping,* are offered to derail a specific substantive bill in the midst of debate, we would code this as a vote on the bill rather than as mere housekeeping.

G. *Quasi-private bills* covers economic benefits to particular individuals and single-named companies, firms, or organizations. No omnibus bill, therefore, can fall in this subcategory, unless amendments to an omnibus bill are made for specific claimants.

H. *Public quasi-private bills* covers specific benefits that are not for individuals or single-named companies but include features of a public good, including building a specific bridge, building and administering individual public buildings, and transferring public property, such as a tract of land, a building, or an office, to a city or county.

Chapter III

Political Polarization and Issues: A New Perspective

MOST CONGRESSIONAL STUDIES, especially empirically based ones, ultimately study political behavior. Because these types of studies typically utilize roll call measures (such as interest group scores, ideal point estimates, roll rates, coalition sizes, and voting behavior on selected votes), the contributions to what we know about the U.S. Congress, as well as the controversies in this field of study, are often closely connected to the analysis and interpretation of roll calls. Roll call votes are relied upon heavily in contemporary work on Congress, but they have been studied seriously by Congress scholars for a very long time. Roll call analyses rose in prominence in the early stages of the behavioral revolution in political science. David Truman, in his book *The Congressional Party* (1959, vii) concisely stated why roll calls are so useful: "The yea-and-nay votes, nevertheless, though enigmatic, are a public record of choices made among measures and men. Their number and regularity make them significant composite indicators of roles. Properly used, they are a protection against an easy tendency to find in the many-faceted Congressional institution illustration of one's prejudices rather than answers to one's objective questions." Truman's words explain why roll call measures have subsequently been used so prominently and so often to investigate many different aspects of Congress.

Although I argue in this book that we must not solely study roll call votes if our purpose is to understand lawmaking, we can without doubt learn much from studying them, primarily because roll call votes provide the best data for measuring the political preferences of members of Congress and understanding preferences is a critical zone of enterprise in the study of Congress. I argue that we have actually underutilized roll calls because most studies that have focused on the induced preferences of members of Congress ignore policy issue substance. This neglect has led to a myopic picture of congressional behavior. This chapter and the next provide a needed correction to the picture of congressional preferences by systematically incorporating policy issue substance into the story. Drawing on a mountain of empirical data, both chapters demonstrate that members have different preferences across issue areas. Through an analysis of political polarization, this chapter demonstrates the substantive importance of this finding.

ESTIMATING INDUCED PREFERENCES OF MEMBERS OF CONGRESS

The empirical work in this chapter is based largely on an analysis of ideal point estimates of members of Congress. Using "ideal points"—or, in the academic terminology, measures of induced preferences of members of Congress—to study the behavior of lawmakers is commonplace in the political arena as well as in academia. These "scores" usually measure the liberal-conservative position of members of Congress. Outside of academia, the scores are simply interpreted as measuring the political preferences of legislators. The most commonly used ideal point scores come from Keith Poole and Howard Rosenthal's NOMINATE project.[1] However, many scholars have drawn on Bayesian methods instead of the NOMINATE method to estimate ideal points. Simon Jackman and Joshua Clinton have been particularly influential in arguing that the Bayesian approach is the preferable method. In particular, Simon Jackman's IDEAL software, which implements the technique explained in Clinton, Jackman, and Rivers (2004), has made it easy to estimate Bayesian-based ideal points. Joshua Clinton and Simon Jackman (2009) argue that neither a Bayesian approach like IDEAL nor Poole and Rosenthal's NOMINATE have clear advantages over the other in estimating ideal points for legislators in either small or large legislatures. Both methods have almost always produced similar results, they point out, "and when they do not, the discrepancy is due to the somewhat arbitrary identification and computational constraints imposed by each method" (Clinton and Jackman 2009, 593). Clinton and Jackman argue, however, that the Bayesian approach is "more flexible than the family of NOMINATE estimators, as it is more easily adapted to account for additional data structures and alternative modeling assumptions" (593). In short, because the Bayesian method is more flexible, is easier to implement, and usually produces similar results to NOMINATE, I use it here for estimating ideal points. Specifically, I generate the estimates using Jackman's IDEAL package (Clinton, Jackman, and Rivers 2004; Jackman 2004).

Overall, I estimate 28,196 ideal points for House members during the period 1877 to 2010 (45th to 111th Congresses) and 6,652 ideal points for senators

---

[1] Poole and Rosenthal's NOMINATE project (Poole and Rosenthal 1985, 1991, 1997) is heavily cited and has received the attention of countless journalists. As of early 2013, Google Scholar turns up 2,194 citations of their book *Congress: A Political-Economic History of Roll Call Voting* (1997) and 583 citations for their article "Patterns of Congressional Voting" (1991).

between 1877 and 1996 (45th to 104th Congresses), in 2001–2002 (107th Congress), and in 2009–2010 (111th Congress).[2] These ideal point estimates are based on a total of 34,281 roll calls for the House and 29,859 for the Senate. Using IDEAL for each Congress, I estimated ideal points for specific issue areas by using only roll calls coded for each issue area. So, for example, in the 89th Congress (one of my case studies in chapter 4) I used all 44 sovereignty votes in the House to estimate sovereignty-specific scores. I used the same method for every issue area and Congress. I also estimated ideal point scores using the entire set of roll call votes for each Congress so that aggregate ideal points (similar to W-NOMINATE scores) could be used for comparison purposes.[3]

One of the issues in using ideal point estimates that are based on voting in a single Congress is that the scaling of legislators for that particular Congress may be influenced by the particular agenda during that session. This makes temporal comparison difficult, as it is unclear whether member estimates across time are driven by the agenda, changes in member preferences, or the introduction of new members into Congress. To deal with this issue, I apply the scaling technique outlined in Groseclose, Levitt, and Snyder (1999) to my estimates by policy issue area. This algorithm allows for across-time comparisons of legislators, similar to DW-NOMINATE. However, there are obvious trade-offs to using such transformations. The biggest problem deals with the fact that the effects associated with the policy agenda of a particular Congress might be wiped out. One might argue that these effects are real, and that wiping them out distorts the politics of particular Congresses. Consequently, the case studies in chapter 4 rely on the static, nontransformed scores, as they allow for the policy agenda of a particular Congress to not be diminished in the estimates of Congress-specific ideal point scores. For the case studies, which are located in a particular Congress, static scores are fine and even preferable. I use the adjusted scores in this chapter, however, because it is necessary to have scores that can be used across time to study political polarization longitudinally.

---

[2] Although I estimate aggregate scores for senators through the 111th Congress, issue-specific coding for the Senate did not exist for the 105th, 106th, 108th, 109th, and 110th Congresses, which thus have not been coded yet by policy issue area (Senate only). Consequently, I have estimated 6,142 issue-specific ideal points. The remaining Congresses are being coded, and issue-specific ideal points will be estimated upon completion and posted online. The Senate polarization graphs show the 45th to 103rd Congresses owing to the fact that the 104th, 107th, and 111th Congresses need to be coded or checked for intercoder reliability for the upper chamber roll calls.

[3] The model I used to estimate ideal points is a one-dimensional model. This differs from the two-dimensional DW-NOMINATE model.

POLITICAL POLARIZATION AND POLICY ISSUE SUBSTANCE

Elite polarization in the United States is a hot topic inside the academy as well as in the political world. Dozens of academic articles and books have been published on the topic, and the subject consistently receives a tremendous amount of media coverage. In fact, cable news is saturated with discussion of the extreme polarization of elections and the negative impact on governance. Scholars have become very interested in this topic over the past decade, and consequently we have learned a great deal empirically about elite polarization. The two most important findings from this literature are that elite polarization in Congress has been steadily increasing from the 1970s to the present, and that polarization has followed a U-shape over the last 130 years. The U-shape portrait shows a very high rate of polarization in the late twentieth century, with a peak in the 1980s and then again in the 2000s. These two findings have been cemented as empirical truths for scholars of Congress. Much research has examined the underlying causes of political polarization as well as its effects on lawmaking, but the starting point of most research on this topic is based on these two key empirical findings.

Nolan McCarty, Keith Poole, and Howard Rosenthal provide, in my opinion, the most complete and compelling account of the polarization literature across time in their book *Polarized America: The Dance of Ideology and Unequal Riches* (2006). They define polarization empirically as the absolute difference between the means of the total numbers of Democratic and Republican members in the House and Senate. This definition, which is now standard in most political science research, is the definition employed in this chapter.[4] McCarty, Poole, and Rosenthal's central finding is that polarization dropped precipitously in both chambers of Congress beginning in the mid-1920s, remained low from the beginning of the New Deal through the early 1970s, then began marching upward. This is shown in figure 3.1.

The conventional wisdom about elite polarization—nicely portrayed in figure 3.1—has never received a serious empirical challenge. This is not to say that all of the empirical analyses on elite polarization are identical. In fact, the picture of congressional polarization changes somewhat when we use other measures of party polarization in lieu of ideal points. For example, using party unity scores instead of NOMINATE to measure polarization, I observe considerably more variation in polarization across time, especially when broken down by party. Party unity scores, of course, are simple indicators of partisan agreement where party unity is defined as a vote that pits a majority of one party against a majority of the opposite party. Partly because of their

---

[4]Scholars sometimes use the difference in medians instead of means. Empirically, the two measures are indistinguishable.

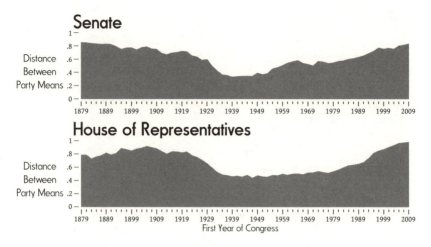

Figure 3.1
Polarization: The House of Representatives and the Senate (DW-NOMINATE), 1879 to 2009

simplicity and intuitive character, these scores have a long history of use in political science research, and this is probably the reason why Poole provides a comparison of party unity scores and NOMINATE-based polarization on his Polarized America website.[5] Poole's party unity figures are replicated in figure 3.2, which shows party unity for the House of Representatives and the Senate between 1877 and 2010.

HOUSE AND SENATE PARTY UNITY SCORES, 1877–2011

It was the fact that the overall upward trend of polarization beginning in the 1970s, combined with a dip in polarization in midcentury America, was reflected in the party unity figures (figure 3.2) that led Poole to write on his website that party unity scores tend to track the NOMINATE polarization figures. My replication places the correlation between party unity scores and DW-NOMINATE at 0.68 for the House of Representatives. Although I agree that this is a reasonably strong correlation, there are some stark Congress-specific differences between the NOMINATE measures and party unity scores. For example, the 75th Congress, which ushered in the second term of President Franklin Roosevelt, shows a different story depending on whether we look at DW-NOMINATE or party unity scores. The NOMINATE scores provide a picture of a moderately polarized Congress. Party unity scores, however, show

---

[5] Available at: http://polarizedamerica.com.

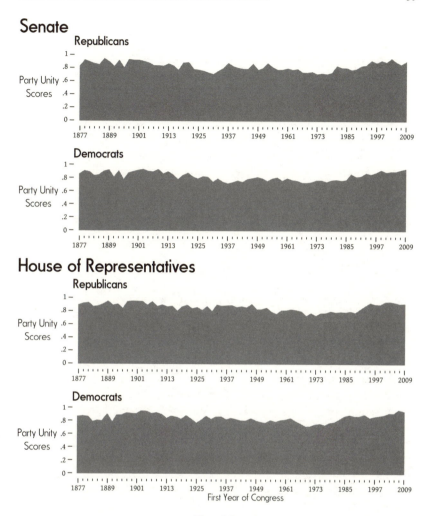

Figure 3.2
Party Unity Scores: The House of Representatives and the Senate, 1877 to 2009

that this was a very polarized Congress. In this particular instance, the truth seems closer to the story told by the party unity scores. The 75th Congress was dominated by the Democratic Party, with the Democratic majority outnumbering Republicans 334 to 88 in the House of Representatives and 76 to 16 in the Senate. Although the Republican Party was reduced greatly in numbers, this small minority was fiercely opposed to Roosevelt's efforts, especially legislation aimed at government organization efforts. This opposition led to a big gap between the congressional Republicans and Democrats. The differences

in this Congress between DW-NOMINATE scores and party unity scores illustrate how the NOMINATE algorithm smoothes across Congresses with the
effect of wiping out specific Congress effects, most likely in relation to what was
on the political agenda. Consequently, NOMINATE is probably best used for
studying longer-term trends in American politics, while measures that draw
upon information from only a particular moment in time, such as party unity
scores, are put to better use in the study of the nuances of specific moments.

In summary, NOMINATE does not always produce a similar story to
other measures of legislative and party behavior. Still, NOMINATE scores
do on average track reasonably well with other traditional measures, such as
party unity scores. The larger unanswered question for this book, however,
is whether policy issue substance matters for studying legislative behavior,
including party polarization.

DISAGGREGATING POLITICAL POLARIZATION

There is without question a substantial gap in the polarization literature,
which includes virtually no empirical work that assesses systematically how
polarization behaves in American politics across policy issue areas. Here I
begin to fill this gap by assessing the question of whether some issue areas
are more polarized than others, comparing aggregate ideal points with issue-
specific ones and addressing questions like: How and when are issue scores
across policy related? And when do they differ?

My study of polarization across time begins with figure 3.3, which
replicates earlier work on polarization by estimating aggregate scores that
draw on all roll call votes for each Congress. Consequently, the ideal points
presented in the figure are similar to DW-NOMINATE scores, though they
certainly are not identical. Like other scholars, I find in the Senate that there
is a sustained period from World War II onward in which polarization
decreases significantly, only to increase significantly beginning in the 1970s
and continuing into the contemporary period. In the House, I find that the
polarization starts decreasing a little later. This is shown for both the House
and Senate in figure 3.3. In summary, the figure shows a story that is somewhat
similar to the one presented by McCarty, Poole, and Rosenthal (2006) as well
as by others. The conventional wisdom is partially replicated in this analysis.
The graphs show an increase in polarization starting in the 1970s through
the contemporary period. There are, however, differences in particular
Congresses. This is particularly evident in the early part of the New Deal.[6]

---

[6]It is important to note that my ideal points are based on a one-dimensional model. Future work
will explore the importance of using a one-dimensional instead of a two-dimensional model.

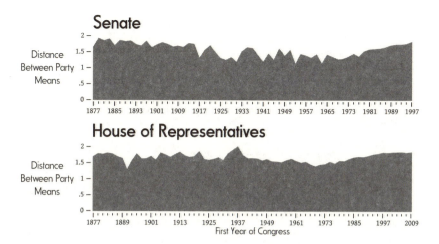

Figure 3.3

Aggregate Polarization: The House of Representatives and the Senate, 1877 to 2009

The traditional U-shaped story of polarization changes dramatically, however, if the evaluation moves to a study of polarization across policy issue areas.[7] This is shown for the four main tier 1 categories in figure 3.4 for the House of Representatives. Specifically, I find that the decrease in polarization starting in the New Deal based on aggregate scores occurs differently across issue areas, in both extent and timing. In the House, sovereignty policy sees an early and dramatic decrease in partisan polarization, first at the turn of the century and then again with the beginning of the New Deal era. International affairs policy sees a reduction in polarization, but it occurs later, during World War II and the onset of the Cold War. It is during the middle of the Cold War period that polarization is relatively low in the House for international affairs. Domestic policy, by contrast, remains relatively polarized throughout the entire time period, decreasing much less than the other issue areas. The finding that domestic policy is consistently polarized in the House across history relative to the other issue areas is striking. In fact, it is a very important finding that suggests that the parties are always apart on domestic issues. This is also true of induced preferences dealing with matters of organization and scope. The two parties are nearly always apart on these issues. This is not to say that there is no variation, but the picture speaks for itself. These portraits

[7]A clear trend across issue scores is the high correlation of the aggregate ideal points with the domestic affairs scores. In fact, the aggregate scores are correlated with the domestic scores at the 0.96 level for the House across the entire period, with very little variation across Congresses. This is not a surprise given that the bulk of roll calls cast are on domestic affairs.

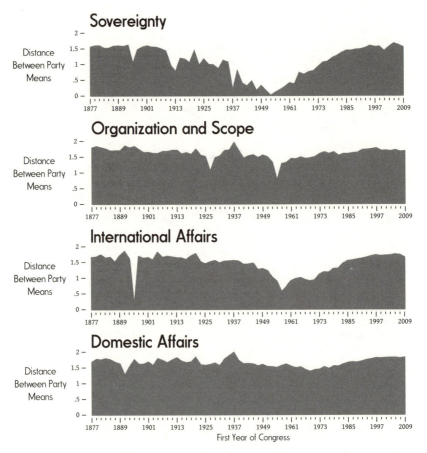

Figure 3.4
The House of Representatives: Tier 1 Polarization, 1877 to 2009

suggest that aggregate party polarization is largely driven by sovereignty policy and foreign affairs. Combined, these findings rewrite the conventional wisdom on political polarization. I would argue that these findings are likely to be counter-intuitive for the many Congress scholars who assume that domestic affairs drives party polarization.

Is a similar pattern present in the Senate? The answer is yes, though with subtle differences. The overall pattern is comparable, albeit reduced, in the Senate. This is not particularly surprising given that the Senate was designed institutionally to be the chamber of Congress that is more stable and less susceptible to large electoral swings. Figure 3.5 shows polarization across tier 1 categories for the Senate. A clear finding shown in figure 3.5 is that prior to the

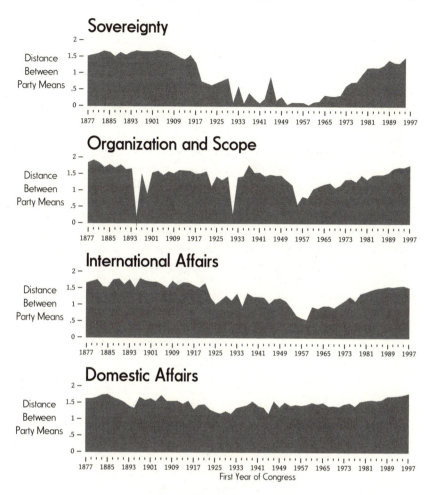

Figure 3.5
The Senate: Tier 1 Polarization, 1877 to 1997

100th (1987–88) Congress, policy issues generate considerable divergence in ideal points. Sovereignty policy polarization is low in the Senate from World War I until the late 1960s. It will be shown in chapter 4 that sovereignty policy is largely driven, not surprisingly, by intraparty splits. We see similar patterns in international affairs and domestic politics across the Senate and House. In international affairs, polarization is modest during a good chunk of the Cold War. The domestic politics finding is striking (just as it was for the House). There is no U-shape or significant rise in domestic polarization beginning in the 1970s—it is always polarized. Given that one might expect the

Senate to be the more moderate of the two chambers, this finding is even more surprising.

If we focus on particular moments, we see Congresses with large divergences across tier 1 policy issue areas. In the extreme, there are several Congresses in which the correlation between sovereignty and domestic issues is under 0.05, including in the House 77th (1941–43) and 78th (1943–45) during World War II and in Eisenhower's 83rd (1953–55) and 84th (1955–57) Congresses.

In these Congresses, members' induced preferences on sovereignty and domestic issues are extremely dissimilar. These are not rare cases. Correlations of below 0.25 across fifteen pairs of issue scores in the House and twenty-four pairs of issue scores in the Senate can be observed across the entire time period, illustrating that issue scores are often very dissimilar across Congresses. Tables 3.A1 and 3.A2 in the chapter appendix provide the correlations across issue areas and with the aggregate Congress-by-Congress scores for the House and Senate. The differences across issue areas will be more fully explored in chapter 4. This correlational analysis simply highlights the fact that issue scores by policy area are not always alike and sometimes are quite dissimilar. This is also obviously reflected in the polarization graphs by issue area in this chapter.

CONCLUSION

The clear consequence of the variation in congressional polarization by policy issue area is that even during times of high polarization at the aggregate level, policymaking in some issue areas might be much less polarized, with potential consequences for legislative accomplishment by policy issue area. The big finding related to the disaggregation of political preferences by policy issue area is that the conventional wisdom surrounding political polarization does not hold across issue areas. The most surprising finding here is that domestic politics is nearly always polarized in both the House and the Senate.

This finding does not suggest that bipartisanship is absent in lawmaking in domestic affairs. It does, however, suggest that polarization is common in domestic affairs across time. This finding, combined with the trends present in sovereignty and international affairs policy, gives us much to think and theorize about in terms of polarization. This is a big topic, of course, but the work here provides an empirical basis on which to begin theorizing about the mechanisms underlying polarization in Congress.

In addition, the demonstration here that the induced preferences of members of Congress vary considerably across policy issues has important implications for how we study political behavior in Congress. These implications are fully explored in more detail as I move to the case studies in the next chapter. Chapter 4 provides a more fine-grained illustration of how variation in induced preferences matters for studying specific cases of lawmaking.

APPENDIX

Table 3.A1 The House of Representatives: Correlation Between Issue Areas (Static Scores)

Congress	Sovereignty Organization	Sovereignty International	Sovereignty Domestic	Organization International	Organization Domestic	Domestic International
45th	0.87	0.83	0.85	0.87	0.87	0.91
46th	0.85	0.84	0.85	0.88	0.89	0.9
47th	0.83	0.83	0.83	0.86	0.87	0.88
48th	0.78	0.79	0.81	0.85	0.87	0.86
49th	0.85	0.86	0.87	0.83	0.86	0.89
50th	0.85	0.83	0.84	0.86	0.84	0.86
51st	0.87	0.85	0.83	0.86	0.87	0.88
52nd	0.74	0.73	0.65	0.85	0.6	0.68
53rd	0.87	0.85	0.72	0.83	0.73	0.7
54th	0.52	0	0.49	0.09	0.73	0.11
55th	0.84	0.82	0.78	0.86	0.8	0.84
56th	0.87	0.89	0.86	0.83	0.86	0.84
57th	0.88	0.86	0.86	0.86	0.87	0.85
58th	0.89	0.89	0.87	0.91	0.9	0.9
59th	0.82	0.79	0.8	0.87	0.88	0.86
60th	0.82	0.83	0.84	0.88	0.87	0.9
61st	0.85	0.83	0.86	0.88	0.89	0.87
62nd	0.45	0.49	0.5	0.85	0.91	0.87
63rd	0.34	0.36	0.44	0.77	0.86	0.82
64th	0.69	0.74	0.71	0.84	0.87	0.86
65th	0.81	0.81	0.82	0.84	0.87	0.85
66th	0.45	0.5	0.51	0.84	0.8	0.86
67th	0.78	0.77	0.83	0.88	0.89	0.91
68th	0.38	0.53	0.46	0.84	0.82	0.84
69th	0.67	0.73	0.74	0.77	0.85	0.83
70th	0.4	0.65	0.72	0.55	0.6	0.84
71st	0.68	0.72	0.68	0.8	0.8	0.82
72nd	0.63	0.59	0.71	0.85	0.80	0.76

Table 3.A1 Continued.

Congress	Sovereignty Organization	Sovereignty International	Sovereignty Domestic	Organization International	Organization Domestic	Domestic International
73rd	0.77	0.79	0.82	0.81	0.89	0.84
74th	0.72	0.74	0.76	0.78	0.76	0.81
75th	0.52	0.55	0.49	0.72	0.86	0.7
76th	0.86	0.76	0.88	0.81	0.9	0.81
77th	0.46	0.37	0.08	0.76	0.69	0.64
78th	0.35	0.02	0.2	0.78	0.83	0.83
79th	0.48	0.23	0.61	0.76	0.9	0.76
80th	0.58	0.38	0.63	0.68	0.89	0.61
81st	0.29	0.24	0.47	0.8	0.87	0.84
82nd	0.75	0.78	0.82	0.84	0.89	0.87
83rd	0.31	0.24	0.15	0.58	0.88	0.66
84th	0.18	0.23	0.06	0.43	0.36	0.51
85th	0.68	0.47	0.44	0.41	0.79	0.14
86th	0.45	0.61	0.15	0.49	0.78	0.32
87th	0.74	0.8	0.74	0.79	0.91	0.85
88th	0.82	0.83	0.84	0.88	0.89	0.89
89th	0.84	0.83	0.83	0.83	0.89	0.87
90th	0.65	0.81	0.75	0.79	0.91	0.87
91st	0.8	0.87	0.88	0.71	0.89	0.8
92nd	0.69	0.88	0.82	0.69	0.89	0.83
93rd	0.73	0.83	0.81	0.83	0.94	0.9
94th	0.81	0.89	0.89	0.85	0.93	0.89
95th	0.9	0.91	0.92	0.86	0.95	0.92
96th	0.85	0.89	0.91	0.86	0.92	0.93
97th	0.89	0.85	0.94	0.78	0.93	0.89
98th	0.85	0.88	0.88	0.81	0.92	0.88
99th	0.84	0.92	0.91	0.86	0.92	0.93
100th	0.89	0.94	0.94	0.91	0.94	0.96
101st	0.89	0.93	0.93	0.88	0.92	0.95
102nd	0.91	0.92	0.93	0.94	0.95	0.96
103rd	0.9	0.91	0.94	0.91	0.95	Domestic
104th	0.93	0.92	0.95	0.92	0.96	0.96
105th	0.88	0.88	0.9	0.93	0.96	0.96
106th	0.89	0.89	0.93	0.9	0.94	0.95
107th	0.82	0.82	0.86	0.88	0.93	0.94

Table 3.A1 Continued.

Congress	Sovereignty Organization	Sovereignty International	Sovereignty Domestic	Organization International	Organization Domestic	Domestic International
108th	0.89	0.89	0.92	0.91	0.94	0.95
109th	0.89	0.92	0.94	0.91	0.93	0.96
110th	0.89	0.9	0.93	0.92	0.93	0.96
111th	0.86	0.83	0.9	0.88	0.95	0.92

Table 3.A2 The Senate: Correlation Between Issue Areas (Static Scores)

Congress	Sovereignty Organization	Sovereignty International	Sovereignty Domestic	Organization International	Organization Domestic	Domestic International
45th	0.75	0.75	0.68	0.85	0.8	0.87
46th	0.85	0.84	0.88	0.93	0.87	0.86
47th	0.85	0.82	0.85	0.9	0.91	0.91
48th	0.82	0.76	0.86	0.73	0.81	0.77
49th	0.87	0.76	0.87	0.79	0.91	0.8
50th	0.78	0.83	0.81	0.89	0.89	0.93
51st	0.8	0.85	0.8	0.88	0.84	0.88
52nd	0.85	0.78	0.72	0.77	0.77	0.71
53rd	0.85	0.88	0.49	0.89	0.51	0.66
54th	0.01	0.6	0.46	0.17	0.41	0.73
55th	0.79	0.82	0.74	0.82	0.78	0.87
56th	0.34	0.88	0.86	0.37	0.39	0.86
57th	0.86	0.82	0.78	0.8	0.75	0.82
58th	0.78	0.85	0.79	0.84	0.78	0.84
59th	0.75	0.71	0.73	0.81	0.78	0.84
60th	0.72	0.78	0.75	0.67	0.83	0.69
61st	0.77	0.8	0.78	0.86	0.86	0.88
62nd	0.78	0.8	0.82	0.87	0.9	0.89
63rd	0.65	0.77	0.62	0.86	0.85	0.79
64th	0.82	0.85	0.85	0.83	0.88	0.87
65th	0.73	0.83	0.39	0.82	0.46	0.47
66th	0.51	0.55	0.46	0.72	0.66	0.61
67th	—	—	—	0.81	0.84	0.83
68th	0.17	0.17	0.37	0.47	0.5	0.79
69th	—	—	—	0.6	0.77	0.7
70th	—	—	—	0.72	0.79	0.75

Table 3.A2 Continued.

Congress	Sovereignty Organization	Sovereignty International	Sovereignty Domestic	Organization International	Organization Domestic	Domestic International
71st	0.48	0.46	0.34	0.82	0.89	0.84
72nd	0.15	0.16	0.45	0.08	0.31	0.71
73rd	0.58	0.51	0.47	0.79	0.82	0.69
74th	0.45	0.31	0.45	0.46	0.63	0.1
75th	0.08	0.07	0.08	0.66	0.84	0.59
76th	0.2	0.06	0.41	0.6	0.71	0.4
77th	0.54	0.53	0.42	0.74	0.75	0.55
78th	0.18	0.08	0.1	0.64	0.79	0.58
79th	0.7	0.76	0.68	0.72	0.79	0.86
80th	0.02	0.15	0.12	0.81	0.88	0.73
81st	0.78	0.76	0.73	0.82	0.85	0.8
82nd	0.42	0.51	0.52	0.8	0.85	0.81
83rd	0.72	0.66	0.74	0.87	0.84	0.77
84th	—	—	—	0.62	0.2	0.24
85th	0.65	0.63	0.05	0.53	0.59	0.02
86th	0.87	0.67	0.44	0.68	0.46	0.24
87th	0.75	0.49	0.44	0.7	0.76	0.82
88th	0.55	0.56	0.38	0.77	0.84	0.76
89th	0.6	0.68	0.66	0.65	0.88	0.72
90th	0.8	0.72	0.75	0.79	0.9	0.79
91st	0.81	0.78	0.72	0.81	0.84	0.84
92nd	0.62	0.74	0.8	0.85	0.9	0.9
93rd	0.82	0.68	0.86	0.88	0.96	0.87
94th	0.73	0.81	0.83	0.83	0.88	0.93
95th	0.79	0.87	0.86	0.85	0.93	0.89
96th	0.78	0.81	0.84	0.86	0.91	0.92
97th	0.85	0.75	0.77	0.76	0.79	0.93
98th	0.82	0.79	0.82	0.84	0.91	0.93
99th	0.85	0.9	0.88	0.9	0.86	0.91
100th	0.73	0.83	0.85	0.85	0.91	0.89
101st	0.78	0.84	0.89	0.8	0.84	0.95
102nd	0.86	0.8	0.89	0.85	0.92	0.9
103rd	0.87	0.84	0.88	0.93	0.95	0.94
104th	0.88	0.82	0.92	0.88	0.95	0.91
107th	—	—	—	0.81	0.82	0.92
111th	0.89	0.91	0.93	0.9	0.92	0.92

The Case Studies: Policy Issue Substance and the Political Behavior of Members of Congress

With David Bateman

THIS CHAPTER EXPLORES in detail the importance of policy issue substance to the study of significant instances of lawmaking across American history. The chapter is divided into two sections. The first section begins with an overview of Poole and Rosenthal's analysis of the 95th Congress (1977–78) and revisits their conclusion that policy issue substance is inconsequental, an interpretation I show to be incorrect. The second section comprises case studies of five tier 1 sovereignty policies, each from a different Congress. The idea behind the case studies is to show how differences across preferences by issue area matter for studying lawmaking. In the case studies, I show that not correctly measuring preferences for specific issues leads to wrong conclusions. I do this analytically by drawing upon common theoretical frameworks in the lawmaking literature to assess the behavior of policymaking in each case studied.

The cases were selected to maximize temporal diversity, to focus the analysis on significant legislation, and to explore variations along two variables recognized as important determinants of legislative productivity: polarization and war. The specific cases are listed in table 4.1, which summarizes the Congresses and specific policies considered here.

REASSESSING THE 95TH CONGRESS

The 95th Congress (1977–78) ushered in unified Democratic government with the election of a little-known outsider, Georgia governor Jimmy Carter. Making good on his pledge to implement a "people's presidency," President Carter established a rocky relationship with Congress, and poor executive-congressional relations, not surprisingly, resulted in only moderate legislative production. According to *New York Times* correspondent Martin Tolchin, the reasons for the lackluster results included "a lack of strong Presidential

Table 4.1 The Five Case Studies

Case/Congress	Date Enacted	Issue Category	Divided	First Term	War
(1) Chinese Exclusion Act (52nd)	May 5, 1882	Membership and nation	Divided (Republication president, Democratic House, Republican Senate)	No	No
(2) Espionage Act (65th)	June 15, 1917	Liberty	Divided (Democratic president, Republican House, Democratic Senate)	No	Yes
(3) Alaska and Hawaii State Admission Act (85th)	July 7, 1958	Boundaries	Divided (Republican president, Democratic House and Senate)	No	No
(4) Alaska and Hawaii State Admission Act (86th)	March 15, 1959	Boundaries	Unified (Democratic)	Yes	No
(5) Voting Rights Act (89th)	August 6, 1965	Civil rights	Unified (Democratic)	No	No

leadership, the complexity of many issues before Congress, the lack of a national consensus and an increased Congressional skepticism over the ability of the Government to improve many national situations."[1]

Although the 95th Congress was not particularly productive, it did distinguish itself by the incredible number of roll call votes cast by both chambers; House members cast an unprecedented 1,540 votes. According to Poole and Rosenthal (1997, 55), this was the only reason why they chose this Congress as an empirical case study to evaluate Aage Clausen's (1973) proposition that different issues produce different roll call scales. Specifically, Clausen found evidence of five distinct "dimensions" to roll call voting.[2] Poole and Rosenthal

[1] Martin Tolchin, "Leaders Call Record of Congress Moderate," *New York Times*, December 18, 1977, p. 38.
[2] James Heckman and James Snyder's (1997) finding that congressional voting is multidimensional (usually three to five dimensions) is often cited as the strongest empirical evidence against

set out to assess Clausen's argument for this particular Congress, but with the idea of generalizing the results to other periods. While Poole and Rosenthal's analysis of the 95th Congress comprises only two pages in their monumental book *Congress: A Political-Economic History of Roll Call Voting*, the findings they report there, combined with their extensive work on the dimensionality of the political issue space, have been very influential for Congress scholars. Their analysis is often used by scholars to justify not bothering with issue-specific measures of induced preference in their analyses of lawmaking. Here I begin to question that assumption by reviewing Poole and Rosenthal's test and findings for the 95th Congress.

Poole and Rosenthal conducted a simple test. They coded roll call votes according to Clausen's five categories: government management, social welfare, agriculture, civil liberties, and foreign and defense policy. They added to Clausen's schema an extra category of miscellaneous policy for unclassifiable roll calls as well as procedural matters and the internal organization of Congress. W-NOMINATE scores were estimated for three of Clausen's categories; civil liberties, agriculture, and miscellaneous policy were lumped together into an omnibus category to enlarge the number of roll calls for estimation purposes. Aside from this arbitrary clustering of issue categories into an omnibus category, the rest of the analysis is intuitive and straightforward. Poole and Rosenthal demonstrate that the 95th Congress is unidimensional and that the "correlations between management, welfare, and residual categories for one-dimensional scalings are all high, around 0.9." "As a whole," they conclude, "the results hardly suggest that each of these clusterings of substantive issues generates a separate special dimension" (Poole and Rosenthal 1997, 55).

Again, the importance of this finding is not confined to the idea of dimensionality. Scholars have broadly interpreted the Poole and Rosenthal findings to mean that issue-specific preferences are similar to aggregate scores. In short, the analysis has been used to justify the use of aggregate-level measures of preferences (comprising all roll call votes) instead of more fine-grained measures. Why use a fine-grained measure if it produces the same result as an aggregate score? There seems to be little doubt that the findings related to dimensionality are robust. However, this does not mean that members of Congress do not possess unique and distinct preferences across issue areas correlated to one or perhaps two underlying political dimensions. This critically important idea, to the best of my knowledge, is not explored by Poole and Rosenthal.

Let's reconsider the 95th Congress. Of the 1,540 House of Representatives roll call votes, we observe 78 sovereignty votes, 203 organization and scope votes, 297 international relations votes, and 889 domestic affairs votes.

---

the low-dimensionality finding of Poole and Rosenthal. It has also been used to suggest that members have distinct preferences across issue areas.

The remaining votes are in the other tier 1 categories. As mentioned earlier, I produced ideal point estimates for individual Congresses, including the 95th, using Jackman's IDEAL software and its Bayesian approach to derive estimates for the tier 1 issue categories of sovereignty, organization and scope, international relations, and domestic affairs. Additionally, I computed aggregate scores using all votes.[3] The ideal point estimates for the 95th Congress across tier 1 categories are all highly correlated with each other. In fact, the correlations between the tier 1 categories and the aggregate range between 0.94 and 0.99. The individual correlations range between 0.86 (organization and scope, international relations) and 0.95 (organization and scope, domestic affairs). In sum, the correlations between issue-specific ideal points are extremely high. In fact, the correlations among our issue categories are even higher than the correlations that Poole and Rosenthal produced in their analysis of the Clausen categories for the 95th House. However, simple correlations can mask substantively important differences in defining the pivotal actors in lawmaking.

The median voter in the House of Representatives is an extremely important member, and identifying who occupies this position is critical for understanding lawmaking in the United States. Figure 4.1 identifies the twenty members of the tier 1 categories who are closest to the median position of the House in the 95th Congress. The figure lists the name of the member, the member's state and district, the member's ideal point estimate, and a 95 percent confidence interval around the ideal point estimate. The ideal point is identified by the dot (the solid circle is for Republicans, and the open circle for Democrats), and the 95 percent confidence interval is the line attached to each ideal point. (The confidence interval simply shows the 95 percent range of where the individual member's ideal point is located.) The results show clearly that different members occupy the position of median voter across issue areas. Not a single member is listed as a median member across all of the tier 1 issue areas. In fact, figure 4.1 shows strikingly that there is very little overlap across the issue-specific scores. The domestic affairs scores overlap with the scores for only three of the median members in the sovereignty and international relations categories, and with those for five median members in the organization and scope category. The organization and scope scores reveal only two median members whose sovereignty scores overlap with this category, and four who overlap in international relations. The international relations scores reveal only a single median member overlapping with the sovereignty scores. The evidence is compelling that issue scores are highly

---

[3] Given that I am studying a particular Congress, I use the static courses that are not adjusted to be comparable across time via the Groseclose et al. (1999) algorithm described in chapter 3. The scores used in the cases are similar to the W-NOMINATE scores employed by Poole and Rosenthal in their analysis of the 95th.

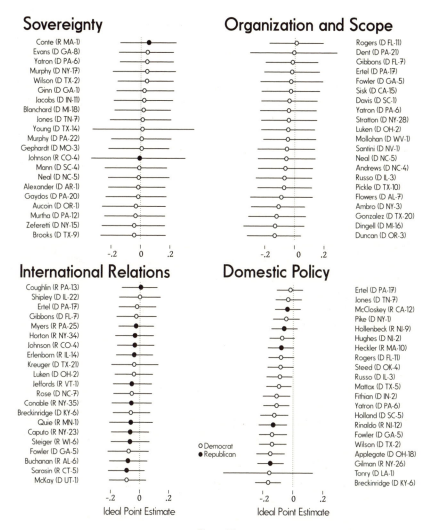

Figure 4.1
Median Members, 95th House of Representatives, 1977 to 1979

correlated with each other, but that different members occupy pivotal positions in the Congress across issue areas.[4]

[4] An analysis of the Senate filibuster pivot for the 95th Congress (not reported here), based on the pivotal politics model of Keith Krehbiel (1998) and David Brady and Craig Volden (1998), shows a similar pattern of very little overlap of members across issue areas.

Thus, our reanalysis of the 95th Congress suggests that it is very important to disaggregate policies by issue area if we want to accurately identify key lawmakers in the policymaking process. This finding is independent of the dimensionality issue. The bottom line is that identifying pivotal members need not be attached to the dimensionality question. More importantly, members' preferences vary in substantively important ways across issue areas even in a low-dimensional political space. This idea will be elaborated upon in the case studies of the next section.

THE CASE STUDIES: EXAMINING SOVEREIGNTY POLICY ACROSS TIME

Congressional scholars are interested not only in the macro trends of legislative productivity and party polarization but also in the micro-level patterns and determinants of legislator behavior. Much of the literature on Congress looks at the formation of voting coalitions around specific legislative agendas. The importance of issue substance in terms of macro trends and legislative outputs explored earlier—that is, the divergence of these trends across issue areas— is embedded in the behavior and preferences of members relative to the temporally specific contexts of political coalitions and legislative agendas. Accordingly, I argue that policy issue substance is a necessary component of any proper understanding of the lawmaking process at the micro level of individual legislators relative to specific legislation within a particular Congress. The goal of this section is to add detail to the claim that policy issue substance matters by focusing on individual member behavior on specific legislation. The following case studies of five pieces of legislation emphasize that our analytical traction in understanding the specific voting coalitions on these bills increases when we pay attention to issue substance relative to when we neglect it.

To support the claim that ignoring policy issue substance limits our under-standing of lawmaking, I show that the magnitude of preference divergence by issue area is sufficiently large that its neglect impairs the performance of otherwise well-supported theoretical models. Accordingly, I present the case studies in the form of analytical narratives—analytical in the sense that they draw explicitly on theoretical models of lawmaking, such as the pivotal politics model and median voter theorem, in their analysis of the policy histories. In tracing the specific trajectories of the laws under consideration, I focus on the "pivotal" legislators specified by these models, drawing on the case histories to assess who is pivotal in particular policy domains and comparing these assessments with the predictions generated using the different measures of legislator ideal points.

I chose the case studies from the sovereignty category of the coding schema. Sovereignty policy is concerned with the key dimensions of citizenship and territory, and sovereignty laws thus constitute an extremely important category of legislation because they define the composition and contours of our nation. These laws have been crucial in structuring the extent of membership in the American political community, the rights and meaning of citizenship, and the extent and control of American territoriality. Empirically, sovereignty legislation is also often characterized by substantial cross-party voting, a factor in members' different preferences in other issue areas, and these cases are broadly illustrative of that type of law. Although it would be hard to generalize from these cases alone, the reader should interpret them with the information provided in the macro-level analysis of polarization, which showed that preferences often diverge across issue areas at particular moments in American history. The moments that show the most divergence often are the ones with the most cross-party voting. It is also important to note that significant legislation often is passed with a considerable degree of cross-party voting (Krehbiel 1998; Mayhew 1991). The cases, then, represent a subset of highly consequential legislative activity.

The cases selected come from all of the four tier 2 subcategories of the sovereignty category: liberty, membership and nation, civil rights, and boundaries. Two cases are drawn from the boundaries category, reflecting the fact that Hawaiian and Alaskan statehood were temporally and substantively linked. I likewise sought to maximize temporal diversity by choosing cases from different historical periods in American political development: the period at the end of the Gilded Age and after the end of Reconstruction, during the height of the Populist revolt (the Chinese Exclusion Act of 1892, passed by the 52nd Congress, 1891–93); the Progressive era, immediately following the outbreak of World War I (the Espionage Act of 1917, passed by the 65th Congress, 1917–19); the Cold War period of divided government under President Dwight Eisenhower (the Alaska and Hawaii Statehood Admission Acts of 1958–59, passed by the 85th and 86th Congresses, 1957–61); and the Great Society and civil rights era (the Voting Rights Act of 1965, passed by the 89th Congress, 1965–67).

As can be seen in table 4.1, the five cases vary along two dimensions recognized as important determinants of legislative productivity: polarization and war.[5] The 52nd and 65th Congresses were held during periods of relatively

---

[5] The Chinese Exclusion Act was the most significant enactment of the 52nd Congress, according to my notability ranking system, which is explained in chapter 5. The Espionage Act was the second most significant law of the 65th Congress, behind the army emergency increase bill, though it also trailed the Prohibition constitutional amendment in overall ranking. The statehood for Alaska bill was the sixth most significant act of the 85th Congress, trailing the National Defense Education Act, the Civil Rights Act of 1957, the Defense Department reorganization, establishment of the

high partisan polarization, while polarization was considerably lower during the 85th, 86th, and 89th Congresses. The 65th Congress convened shortly after the beginning of World War I, while the 85th and 86th took place during the height of the Cold War and only shortly after the end of the Korean War. The 89th Congress convened during the Cold War, near the beginning of the period of détente.

The case studies illustrate instances where individual member–level preferences diverge by issue substance; they are not intended to provide comprehensive coverage of the politics and trajectories of each of the bills considered. Nor do I claim that consequentially distinct preferences and patterns of lawmaking can be seen in all legislation relative to other issue areas. The intent is more limited: to explore more closely whether the principal actors believed that the relevant policy was a distinct issue area in which the considerations of the specified policy were dominant, and to see whether we can find empirical support at a closer level of analysis for the claim that aggregating across issue areas limits our understanding of lawmaking. Finally, the cases supplement the comprehensive and systematic macro-level work in the previous chapter.

The Chinese Exclusion Act of 1892

The Chinese Exclusion Act of 1892, a landmark law passed by the 52nd Congress, extended the Exclusion Act of ten years prior. Not only was it the most notable law passed, according to the significance rankings of chapter 5, in the 52nd Congress, but it is one of the most important immigration laws in the history of the United States, with long-term consequences for patterns of immigration to this country. The Chinese Exclusion Act redefined the exclusion of Chinese on the grounds of "race" rather than nationality and involved the United States in an international dispute with China. The act prohibited the entry of any Chinese laborer into the United States, stipulated that currently residing Chinese were not to be allowed back into the United States if they left, and required Chinese laborers to apply for a certificate of residency. Failure to carry the permit was punishable by hard labor and deportation.

National Space Program, and a trade agreement extension act. Statehood for Hawaii was the fourth most notable act of the 86th Congress, trailing the Act to Prevent Certain Abuses in Labor Organizations, the Civil Rights Act of 1960, and the Social Security Amendments of 1960. The Voting Rights Act of 1965 was ranked third in terms of significance for the 89th Congress, right behind the act to establish Medicare and the Elementary and Secondary School Act. In short, we chose the most significant sovereignty act for each Congress, except for the statehood laws for Alaska and Hawaii: there was a single civil rights bill in each Congress that surpassed these two statehood bills in terms of significance. A desire for variation across sovereignty bills made it important to not select based on significance alone.

Chinese immigration had already been greatly restricted by the Chinese Exclusion Act of 1882, and there was broad support for the goal of "absolutely" restricting Chinese immigration. Much of the controversy centered on whether the act would violate American treaties with China—primarily by excluding Chinese merchants. Nonetheless, both its supporters and its opponents understood the bill as structuring core features of American sovereignty. Supporters were concerned with ensuring the right to exclude certain groups from U.S. territory and saw the exercise of this sovereign power as legitimated on racial grounds. The Chinese Exclusion Acts not only saw the invocation of sovereignty as a basis for exclusion but also shaped American understandings about the basis and limits of sovereignty.

The 52nd Congress met during the last two years of the Benjamin Harrison administration and sat in two sessions from December 7, 1891, to March 3, 1893. It was a divided government, with a Democratic majority in the House (238 Democrats, 86 Republicans, and 8 Populists), a Republican majority in the Senate (47 Republicans, 39 Democrats, and 2 Populists), and a Republican administration. It was a highly polarized and relatively unproductive Congress. Figure 4.2 is a parallel coordinates plot that visualizes changes in ideal point estimates for every member of the 52nd House. Each line represents a member of Congress and tracks their ideal points across each tier 1 category. Member preferences in this Congress are clearly related, but there is also a significant overlap between the parties on sovereignty policy and domestic politics, in contrast to the stark partisan divide seen in organization and scope and international relations and in the aggregate estimates.[6]

Sovereignty policy did not have an equal impact on issue preferences the two parties. This is seen in figure 4.2, a scatter plot of the aggregate estimates against the sovereignty-specific estimates for each party. The aggregate position is a reasonably good predictor of a member's location on sovereignty policy for the Congress as a whole, with a correlation between the members' aggregate and sovereignty-specific ideal points of 0.83. This high correlation, however, obscures the differences between the parties. The aggregate ideal point is a good predictor of a Democratic member's ideal point on sovereignty policy, but is much weaker for the Republicans. For Democrats, the correlation between members' aggregate and sovereignty-specific ideal points is 0.74. For Republicans, the correlation is 0.20. In the 52nd Congress, it was the Republican Party whose preferences on sovereignty diverged considerably from Republican members' preferences on other issues.

The aim of the bill was to renew the Chinese Exclusion Act of 1882, while strengthening the restrictive provisions, notably by restricting all persons of

---

[6]For presentation purposes, independents are excluded from this visualization; however, their inclusion does not change the interpretation of the plot.

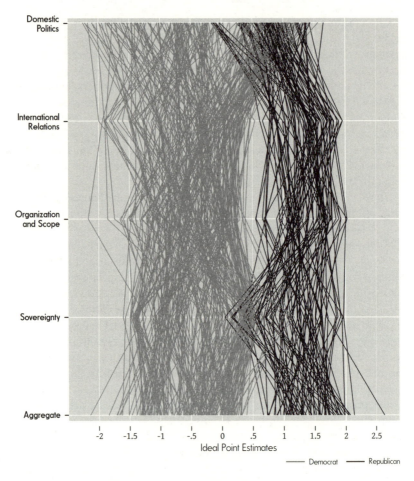

Figure 4.2
Ideal Point Estimates, 52nd House of Representatives, 1891 to 1893

Chinese descent rather than nationality and by imposing a registration system for Chinese laborers. Deciding whether the registration requirement would extend to all Chinese or just Chinese laborers would be a central dispute, as introduced by California Democrat Thomas J. Geary. Despite amendments in 1884 and 1888, contemporary observers had believed that there was insufficient support among eastern groups for the "absolute" prohibition desired by organized western groups. Yet while easterners may have become more sympathetic by 1892, the primary dividing lines in Congress remained regional. Passage of the bill involved some partisan division—Democrats were

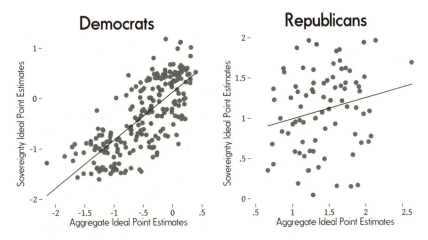

Figure 4.3
Ideal Point Scatter Plot by Party, 52nd House of Representatives, 1891 to 1893

more likely to support exclusion than Republicans—but it is best analyzed as a regionally driven bill: unanimous support in the West was met with some opposition in the Northeast, Midwest, and South. There were factions within both parties that opposed the bill, but the impact was greater on the Republicans. Western Republicans were unanimous in support of the bill, while Northeast Republicans split 53 percent for and 47 percent against and the midwestern Republicans opposed the bill by a margin of 65 percent. By contrast, House Democrats saw 89 percent of midwestern members and 74 percent of northeastern members support the bill.

The driving force behind the legislation was the desire of western members of Congress to absolutely exclude Chinese persons from entering the country; the primary objection stressed by the opposition was the likely disruption of diplomatic relations and reduced trade with China if the bill passed. The scattered southern opposition expressed concern that the abrogation of the treaties would lead to Chinese restrictions on the importation of cotton; Democratic representative Wilkinson Call of Florida argued that the bill would "cause a loss of hundreds of millions to the already crippled cotton industry of the South."[7]

Despite the economic and diplomatic concerns of the opposition, all parties understood that policy was concerned with core features of sovereignty, especially the ability to racially restrict entry into American territory. Supporters of exclusion considered it primarily an issue of controlling entry into the United

---

[7]"Revised Chinese Exclusion Bill," *New York Times*, May 4, 1892, p. 3.

States, based explicitly on racial understandings of American sovereignty. Westerners in Congress argued for further restrictions on the grounds that "these Chinese form an exception in every respect to all races of people who seek our shores."[8] Likewise, the opposition sought to rhetorically support the need to "stem the tide" of "Mongolian immigration" while reframing the debate as a matter of respecting American international treaties.[9]

Treating the Chinese Exclusion Act as pertaining to a specific policy issue area allows us to better identify the pivotal members and more accurately predict a member's position on the legislation. One approach in assessing the relative strengths of different estimates is to use the ideal points to predict specific votes of members of Congress, using a linear or probit regression. For the Chinese Exclusion Act, I estimated two simple probit models, with the roll call vote serving as the dependent variable and the ideal point as the lone independent variable. One model was constructed using aggregate ideal points, the other using sovereignty estimates.[10] Both the aggregate and sovereignty estimates excluded the roll calls on the Chinese exclusion bill for this particular analysis.[11] From these I generated predicted probabilities for members' votes, then compared these probabilities to their actual votes. If the predicted probability was below 0.5 and the member voted against the bill, or if the predicted probability was above 0.5 and the member voted for passage, I coded this as a correct prediction. All others were coded as incorrectly predicted.

The probit results are reported in table 4.A1 in the appendix to the chapter. Of the 221 members who voted on final passage in the House, aggregate estimates correctly predict 174, while sovereignty-specific estimates correctly predict 178. This is a modest increase—and one entirely concentrated among the Republicans. Both estimates correctly predict 148 Democrats (86 percent of voting Democrats), but the sovereignty-specific estimates correctly predict 23 of the 42 voting Republicans (55 percent), compared to 19 (45 percent) for the aggregate estimates. Using aggregate estimates also suggests that the Populist members were likely to be in the median position, where they could play a pivotal role arbitrating between competing proposals. In fact, the 8 Populists in the House voted consistently for stronger exclusionary laws, reflecting the movement's broader antipathy toward immigration. So while the absolute distance between the median Populist and the median of the House using aggregate estimates was 0.0735 (7.4 percent of a standard deviation),

---

[8] 23 *Congressional Record* 2915 (1892).

[9] "Revised Chinese Exclusion Bill," *New York Times*, May 4, 1892, p. 3.

[10] This analysis is a simplified version of the types of regressions presented in Poole and Rosenthal (1997, 122).

[11] The specific roll calls associated with the bill are removed from the sovereignty ideal point estimates so that the same votes are not used to explain each other.

the distance was 0.525 using sovereignty estimates (52.5 percent of a standard deviation).

Many observers believed that the passage of the Geary bill in the House was a political maneuver meant to embarrass the Republican Senate and president. When the bill went to the Senate, it was referred to the conservative Committee on Foreign Relations, which reported back a weaker bill that effectively renewed the 1882 act; it quickly passed. The conference, however, saw the incorporation of various restrictions that were insisted upon by the House, including the denial of bail in all habeas corpus cases, a certificate of residence requirement for Chinese laborers, and a provision that placed the burden of proof on the arrestee. A number of senators switched from having supported the Senate substitute bill to opposing the more restrictive conference report. Of the fifteen senators who switched their position, eight came from the South, while four came from New England, underscoring the regional basis for support and opposition to further restrictions.

In 1889 the Supreme Court decided that the ability to "exclude aliens from its territory" was an "incident of sovereignty belonging to the government of the United States" (*Chae Chan Ping v. United States*, 130 U.S. 581 [1889]). For Justice Stephen Field, unregulated immigration "threatened both the territorial security of the American state... and its racial and cultural composition," according to Alexander Aleinikoff (2012, 14). "Sovereignty meant more than control of borders. It also implied power to construct an 'American people' through the adoption of membership rules." This theme was echoed by advocates of exclusion such as California lawyer H. N. Clement, for whom the exclusion of Chinese was crucially tied to the sovereign rights of the United States: "Have we any right to close our doors against one nation and open them to another? Has the Caucasian race any better right to occupy this country than the Mongolian?" Clement's answer to both questions was yes (Lee 2002, 39).

The Chinese Exclusion Act of 1892 was both supported and opposed by cross-party coalitions, and while its opponents worried about the impact on trade and foreign relations, both supporters and opponents articulated an understanding of the sovereign right of the American nation to exclude on the basis of racial undesirability. They clearly articulated their understanding of the issue as relating to core elements of American sovereignty and, especially among the Republicans, held distinct preferences that are poorly captured by aggregating across issue areas. Relying on aggregate ideal points to understand this important enactment would paint a misleading picture. In short, policy issue substance matters here.

The Espionage Act of 1917

The 1917 Espionage Act was a landmark law passed by the 65th Congress shortly after the entrance of the United States into World War I. In the

1916 elections, the Democrats had narrowly retained the presidency and a majority in the Senate (54 to 42). The Republicans had a plurality in the House (215 seats), but it was organized by a working coalition of Democrats (214), Progressives (3), and independents (3). Despite the relatively high levels of partisan polarization for this Congress, contemporary observers agreed that the conduct of the parties during the first two sessions was not acrimonious or particularly partisan.[12]

The act greatly expanded the authority of the federal government and executive branch, restricting the material that could be delivered through the mail and criminalizing activities aimed at encouraging the obstruction of military recruitment or conveying "false reports or false statements with intent to interfere with the operation or success of the military or to promote the success of its enemies." The act embodied a broad increase in federal power to regulate speech and was widely recognized as such by contemporary observers (Hough 1918, 696). Representing a central component of the Wilson administration's war effort, the bill legislated a core feature of sovereignty, namely, the civil liberties and political rights of American citizens. It was substantive concerns over the potential infringement of the First Amendment that most aroused passions in Congress.

Immediately upon consideration of the bill, controversy erupted over a section restricting the right to publish material in violation of regulations that were to be promulgated by the president. Republican senator William Borah of Idaho insisted that "this establishes a censorship" and asked, "Under what authority do we do that?"[13] Senator Henry Cabot Lodge, Republican from Massachusetts, agreed with Borah's claim, as did progressive Republican senator Hiram Johnson from California. The concern was by no means limited to Republicans; Democratic senators Gilbert Hitchcock of Nebraska and Charles Thomas of Colorado argued that the bill was in all probability unconstitutional. The Democratic Speaker of the House, James "Champ" Clark of Missouri, expressed fundamental concern about the institutions of republican government: "A great many great Americans were opposed to adopting the Constitution on the ground that it had every facility in it for finally making the Federal Government a despotism. [Jefferson] said that he had rather live in a country with a free press and no government than to live in a country with a government and with no free press. And I say the same thing here today."[14] Bipartisan unease with the bill continued as the controversy over what became known as the "censorship provision" mushroomed. The Democratic Speaker and the Republican minority leader, James Mann of Illinois, would both condemn the section, and both Democratic

---

[12] "The Record of Congress," *New York Times*, October 7, 1917, p. 26.
[13] 55 *Congressional Record* 779 (1917).
[14] 55 *Congressional Record* 1764 (1917).

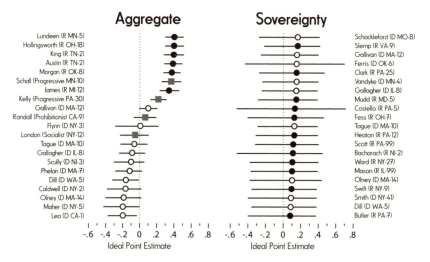

Figure 4.4
Median Members, 65th House of Representatives, 1917 to 1919

and Republican members came to its defense. On May 4, the House voted to strike the section—fifty-three Democrats voted against and twenty-eight Republicans voted with the administration—but a revised version of the section was quickly passed after some representatives had left the House.

This issue saw distinct preferences relative to other issue areas, with distinct voting constellations that are obscured by aggregated ideal point measures and could lead to incorrect inferences regarding the pivotal actors. Figure 4.4 plots the ideal point estimates of the twenty representatives surrounding the median member.[15]

There is some overlap, such as with Representatives Isaac Bacharach (R-NJ-2), James Gallivan (D-MA-12), Thomas Gallagher (D-IL-8), Clarence Cleveland Dill (D-WA-5), and Richard Olney (D-MA-14), but there is also considerable difference between the lists generated using the different policy issue areas. Importantly, the aggregate estimates would predict that the third-party members, such as Thomas Schall (Progressive-MN-10), Clyde Kelly (Progressive-PA-30), Charles Randall (Prohibitionist-CA-9), and Meyer London (Socialist-NY-12), would be relatively indifferent, as median members, to whether an espionage bill had a censorship provision or not. In fact, these members consistently voted against the censorship provision and on this issue should be understood as being well within the coalition that opposed

---

[15] During the period in which the Espionage Act was debated, there were 431 sitting members in the House. The median member is centered on the 215th member.

the provision, not aligned with the median members who were successful in securing its passage in the House.

Given the balance in the House and the opposition to the legislation among Progressives and a sizable contingent of the Democratic caucus, the administration would have needed to secure a considerable number of Republican votes in order to advance the legislation. Using aggregated estimates in a probit model, not a single Republican House member is predicted to vote for censorship provision. Using sovereignty-specific estimates, however, allows us to identify a number of Republican representatives whose preferences on sovereignty policy were substantially distinct from their preferences on other issue areas and whose support was crucial for getting the censorship provision through the House. Figure 4.5 visualizes changes of member preferences by issue area, once again in a parallel coordinates plot. Each member of the 65th House is represented by a line, allowing easy comparison of individual members in relation to the House as a whole. Note the group of Republicans whose ideal points on sovereignty vary significantly from their ideal points using the aggregate measure. The Republicans whose sovereignty estimates diverge significantly from their aggregate estimates formed a crucial bloc of voters who opposed striking the censorship provision from the bill and many of whom supported its reinsertion. Notable among this group were Richard Parker (R-NJ-9), who goes from being the 247th ranked member of the House to the 91st when we use sovereignty-specific ideal points rather than aggregate estimates, as well as Leonidas Dyer (R-MO-12), William Griest (R-PA-9), Ira Copley (R-IL-11), Edgar Kiess (R-PA-15), and Joseph Cannon (R-IL-18). Each of these representatives goes from being on the right side of the median to being either on the left or very close to the median when we switch from aggregate to sovereignty-specific ideal points.

In order for the bill to be passed by the House, twenty-eight Democrats had to change their vote for the revised section. If we rely on the aggregate estimates, these switchers are widely dispersed across the left side of the median. Using the sovereignty-specific estimates, however, the members who changed their vote on the censorship provision are closer to the House median, going from an absolute distance.

The opponents of the provision in the Senate likewise connected their policy positions with their understanding of the rights and values of American citizenship. Progressive senators such as Borah and Johnson, as well as conservative Democrats such as Oscar Underwood of Alabama, spoke against the censorship provision.[16] The vote in the Senate saw "party lines wiped out" as sixteen Democrats and twenty-three Republicans voted to eliminate

---

[16] 55 *Congressional Record* 2116 (1917).

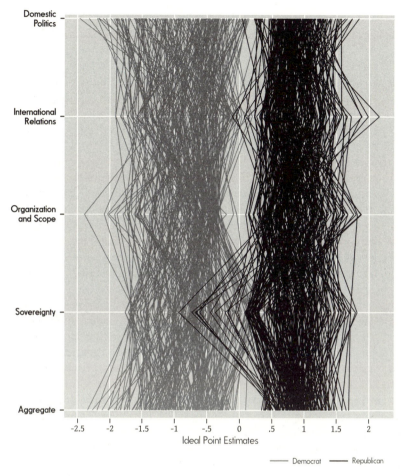

Figure 4.5
Ideal Point Estimates, 65th House of Representatives, 1917 to 1919

the provision while twenty-seven Democrats and eleven Republicans voted to maintain it.[17]

Using the sovereignty-specific ideal point estimates allows us to provide a somewhat more coherent structure to the pattern of voting. For instance, there were a number of Democratic senators—John Bankhead of Alabama, Kenneth McKellar of Tennessee, Robert Broussard of Louisiana, and John Shields of Tennessee, among others—who voted to strike the provision but

---

[17]"Censorship Vote 39 to 38: Party Lines Wiped Out in Line-up on Press Control," *New York Times*, May 13, 1917, p. 1.

who were, according to aggregated estimates, significantly to the left of the median and clustered with the supporters of the administration. When we use a sovereignty-specific estimate, however, these senators are much closer to the median of the chamber, suggesting that their preferences on this issue are not well captured by aggregated estimates.[18] The ideal point estimates do not perfectly explain the voting patterns of the members on this issue, but they do capture more of the variation as we move from the aggregated estimates to the tier 1 sovereignty estimates, and more again as we move to the tier 2 liberty estimates.

The expectation that the conference would report back some form of censorship provision led to a consolidation of House Republican opposition, while administration pressure was expected to move some Democrats to support it. Rights of citizenship remained central to the opposition's attack on the provision, with Republicans arguing that "it is a fundamental principle and the underlying doctrine of this free Government that there shall be free speech and a free press."[19] Nonetheless, it was expected that "the censorship fight is not to be partisan."[20] The crucial vote came in the House, which voted on May 31 to recommit the bill to the conference committee with instructions to agree to eliminate the controversial section. The final vote was 184–144 to strike the provision, with 10 Republicans joining the majority of Democrats in support of the provision and 36 Democrats siding with the opponents. The 10 Republicans voting to maintain the provision included Parker (NJ-9), Dyer (MO-12), and Griest (PA-9), as well as Charles Fuller (IL-12) and William La Follette (WA-4).

The Espionage Act was understood by the participants to fall into a distinct issue area concerning a core feature of sovereignty policy. The divisions cut through both parties and were based on conflicting understandings of how the provision related to, and whether it violated, core tenets of American citizenship. Understanding the dynamics of lawmaking on this issue is best accomplished by recognizing that it took place in a substantively unique issue area, one whose centrality to beliefs about American national identity and citizenship made it likely to generate distinct preferences among members. This recognition is obscured by the use of aggregated ideal point measures and an inattention to policy substance.

---

[18]Using aggregated estimates to rank the distribution of senators, Bankhead is the fifteenth member from the left, McKellar the nineteenth, Broussard the twenty-third, and Shields the twenty-sixth. Using the sovereignty-specific ideal points estimates, however, Bankhead becomes the forty-second, McKellar the thirtieth, Broussard the forty-first, and Shields the forty-third.
[19]55 *Congressional Record* 3134 (1917).
[20]"Say Censorship Will Be Defeated: Senators and Representatives in Private Discussions Condemn Revival of Project," *New York Times*, May 25, 1917, p. 1.

Hawaii and Alaska Statehood

President Eisenhower's second term happened during the 85th (1957–58) and 86th (1959–60) Congresses. Although government was divided under both Congresses, the Democrats saw huge gains in their numbers from the 1958 election. In the 85th, the Democrats maintained a slight numerical edge over Republicans in the Senate (49 to 47) and enjoyed a more comfortable advantage in the House (234 to 201). The Democratic majorities ballooned in the 86th, with 65 to 35 in the Senate and 283 to 153 in the House. One consistency between these two Congresses is that the Democrats dominated southern politics. In a thirteen-state South, Democrats controlled all 26 Senate seats in both Congresses. In the 85th, the 26 southern Democrats made up 53 percent of the Democratic majority. The South's power was particularly influential in the Senate. Using a legal-institutional definition of the South, the region grows to seventeen states. In these seventeen states, legal segregation had been mandated by law when *Brown v. Board of Education* (1954) was adjudicated by the Supreme Court. The states were the fifteen that practiced slavery when the Civil War began, plus West Virginia and Oklahoma. These seventeen states had outlawed interracial marriage just prior to the Supreme Court's decision in *Loving v. Virginia* (1967), which ruled that such laws are unconstitutional.[21] Under a seventeen-state South, the potential for even stronger legislative power over racial matters was present, especially in the Senate with the filibuster (Wawro and Schickler 2004).[22]

The South prized its role as a consequential player in national legislative politics (Katznelson, Lapinski, and Bateman 2012; Katznelson, Geiger, and Kryder 1993). The structural veto given to the South in the Senate could be diluted, however, by expanding the Senate through state admission. The admission of new states has usually been a highly charged sectional and partisan matter across most of American history because state and partisan power has always been a concern in Senate representation. The admission of states with small populations has had only a marginal impact in the House, but the impact is much greater in the Senate. Following the Civil War, the sectional dispute over the admission of new states that had split the Whigs and Democrats was absorbed into the party cleavage as the Republicans sought to maintain their control over the institutions of the federal government

---

[21] The eleven-state South consists of Alabama, Arkansas, Florida, Georgia, Louisiana, Mississippi, North Carolina, South Carolina, Tennessee, Texas, and Virginia. The thirteen-state South adds Kentucky and Oklahoma. The seventeen-state South adds Delaware, Maryland, West Virginia, and Missouri.

[22] Of course, the South had great power in the House of Representatives. The lack of party competition in the South, especially in the eleven-state version, combined with the seniority system that governed powerful House committee assignments, led to southern dominance in committee chairs between the New Deal and the reform era of the early 1970s.

(Stewart and Weingast 1992). Votes on state admission were for the most part predictable straight party votes: Republicans supported statehood for those states seen as being reliably Republican, Democrats supported it for those, such as Utah and Arizona, that were expected to be Democratic in inclination, and both parties opposed the admission of states that would alter the balance in the other's favor.[23]

By the time the question of Alaskan and Hawaiian statehood had returned to the agenda following World War II, however, a different voting pattern had emerged. The Alaskan statehood bill of 1958 was supported by most Democrats and a large number of Republicans, and the same pattern held for the 1959 votes on Hawaiian statehood. The Republican support for what was considered a Democratic territory is explained in part by the party's view that it would facilitate the entrance of Hawaii, which was seen as a Republican territory (although a greater number of Republicans supported the Hawaiian statehood bill than the Alaskan measure).[24] Both parties were split on the issue. Instead of following the prevailing pattern of straight considerations of partisan advantage, the Hawaii-Alaska bills took on the added dimensions of southern opposition and a Republican split.[25]

In the histogram of the induced preferences of members by party shown in figures 4.6 (85th Congress) and 4.7 (86th Congress), we can see the split between southern and northern Democrats. The histogram uses a thirteen-state definition of the South. The major finding shown in both figures is that the sovereignty-specific estimates show southern Democrats to be extreme outliers from their northern Democratic counterparts, and also more conservative on average than Republicans. This is not apparent in the aggregate estimates that

[23]There were some important exceptions to the general trend of Republican support for and Democratic opposition to admission. The bill that brought in Montana, Washington, and the Dakotas was prepared and passed while the Democrats controlled the House and presidency. The Democrats, however, had recently been defeated in 1888 and would soon turn over control of the House and presidency to the Republicans. Thus "compelled to act," the Democrats "used the lame duck session to avoid something worse" (Wirls 1999, 14). There were also Republicans who lamented the influx of western senators and who believed that they had undermined the ability of the Republicans to ensure voting protections for African Americans. Senator John Spooner of Wisconsin, following the defeat of the Force Bill and its replacement by a free coinage bill, wrote: "We are fallen upon bad times for the party. The Confederacy and the western mining camps are in legislative supremacy. Think of it—Nevada, barely a respectable county, furnished two senators to betray the Republican party and the rights of citizenship for silver. We are punished for making too easy the pathway of rotten boroughs into the Union" (15).

[24]Allen Drury, "Alaska and Hawaii Again Losing Statehood Fight, " *New York Times*, p. E7.

[25]Historically, the Republicans were generally less favorable to both projects, although the West was generally more supportive of Hawaiian statehood. Only a few votes during the Congresses in which statehood was considered had strong straight party votes—specifically a vote in the 83rd Senate to decide the question of statehood that had split the Democrats between North and South and aligned the vast majority of Republicans with northern Democrats.

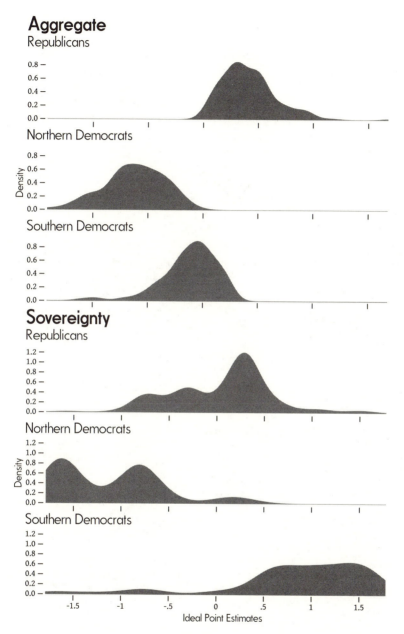

Figure 4.6
Distribution of Ideal Point Estimates, 85th House of Representatives, 1957 to 1959

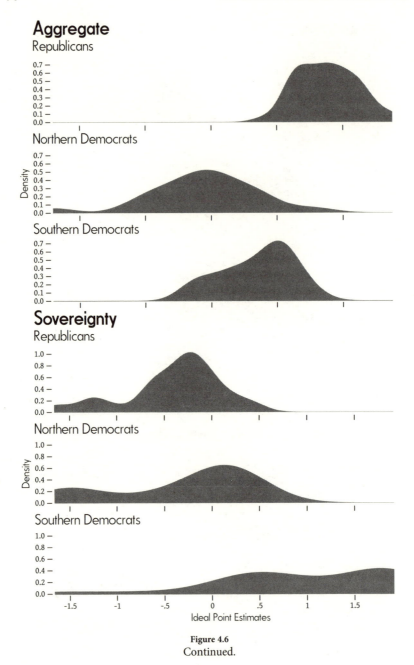

Figure 4.6
Continued.

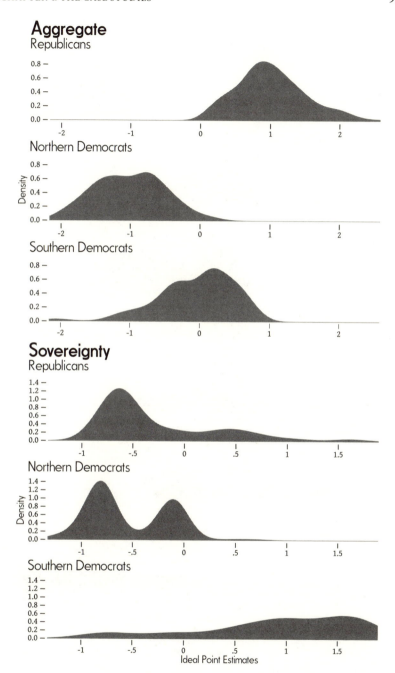

Figure 4.7
Distribution of Ideal Point Estimates, 86th House of Representatives, 1959 to 1961

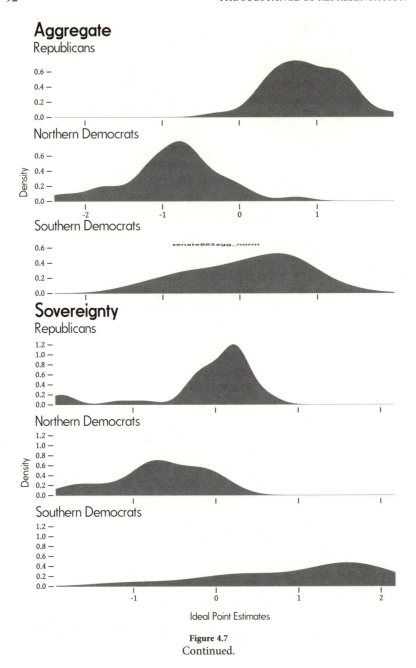

Figure 4.7
Continued.

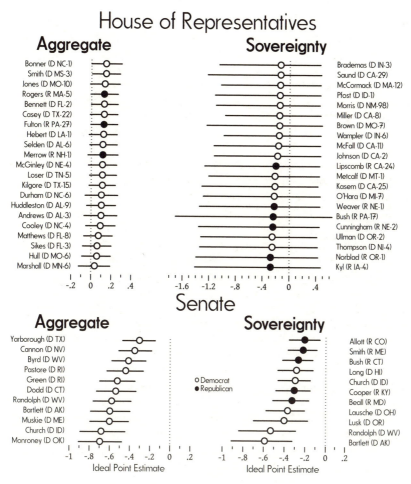

Figure 4.8
Pivotal Members, 86th Congress, 1959 to 1961

show southern Democrats to be centrists near the median of the chamber. The aggregate estimates clearly do an inferior job in explaining the lawmaking process for Alaska and Hawaii state admission.

In the crucial votes on Hawaiian statehood in the 86th Congress, the median members of the House did not seem to be central to the outcome: many of the median members voted against the bill, which passed 323–89. Figure 4.8 shows the House median position for the 86th Congress as well as the filibuster position for the Senate. The House portion of the figure is particularly informative. It shows that 16 of the 20 members surrounding the median position for the aggregate ideal points were from the thirteen-state South. However, the sovereignty-specific ideal points show only one southern member, Charles Brown of Missouri. In fact, southerners were the bloc most likely to oppose statehood. Of the members who voted against final passage, 74 came from the thirteen-state South, and five of them were Republican. Given that only 44 southern members supported the final passage vote, it is clear that the aggregate estimates are inferior measures for understanding this particular case of lawmaking.[26] The effect of measuring policy issue substance is large here.

The consistent pattern of cross-party voting and the ideal points for the 85th and 86th Congresses reveal that state admission had ceased to be a purely partisan matter, although partisan considerations were clearly paramount in the efforts to link the bills and in the timing of their passage. So why had the partisan advantage of additional seats in the Senate ceased to be the dominant factor in the voting behavior of congressmen? The answer, it seems, is that state admission had been absorbed into the growing sectional conflict in the Democratic Party and the growing split between moderate and conservative Republicans. While most Democrats outside of the South supported both bills, most southern Democrats joined with conservative Republicans to oppose them. One reason given by the southerners was concern over the racial composition of Hawaii. The *Los Angeles Times* addressed the claim that "Hawaii's racial intermixture [has been] used as an argument against her entry" in an editorial of March 14, 1950: "Likely enough, Hawaii will send a Senator Watanabe to Washington. What's so bad about that? Members of the Congress include all the strains which make up America, Poles, English, Negroes, Irish, German, American Indian, French, Italian, so forth and so on."[27] Additionally, opponents of statehood for Hawaii charged that the island was under the control of the Communists. "As far as Hawaii is concerned," claimed Rep. Edward Cox of Georgia, "we are creating a

---

[26] Earlier votes on Hawaiian statehood in previous Congresses had seen an even less important role for the median members. The situation was similar in the Senate, where Democrat solidarity was low owing to southern defection. In the 83rd Senate, the final passage vote was 60–34, and it was not the senators centered on the filibuster pivot but Senator James Eastland of Mississippi who threatened to filibuster the bill. This number includes paired votes. The presumed reasoning for Senator Eastland's "slight filibuster" was the belief that the new senators would support civil rights legislation. Eighty percent of senators to the left of the filibuster pivot supported final passage, as did 64 percent to the right. When the Hawaiian bill finally passed in the 86th Senate, only a few conservative Republicans and nearly half of the southern Democrats voted against it.

[27] Representative Henry Larcade of Louisiana, a supporter of statehood, felt that it was necessary to assure the House that he could find no "racial grounds" for denying statehood to Hawaii, saying that the different groups lived together "in perfect harmony. If that is their way of life, that is their business." He added that "the people of the South only ask that they be permitted to deal with their own racial problems in their own way" (C. P. Trussell "Hawaii Statehood Gains in House," *New York Times*, March 7, 1950, p. 1).

State that we know is Communist controlled. When we admit Hawaii we are accepting into the sisterhood of States a community that Harry Bridges [the head of the longshoremen's union] dominates as completely as if it were his child."[28]

The most important reason for blocking Hawaiian and Alaskan statehood, however, was the recognition that the addition of four senators would dilute the southern bloc's influence. In threatening a filibuster, Senator Eastland proclaimed that the admission of Hawaii would mean "two votes for socialized medicine,... two votes for Government ownership of industry; two votes against all racial segregation, and two votes against the South on all social matters." The gentleman from Mississippi was certain that the additional senators would support the use of the federal government to "destroy our dual schools, our social institutions and harmonious racial relationships" (Paul 1975, 145).

Since the Civil War, the extension of statehood to American territories had been inextricably linked with considerations of partisan advantage, especially in the Senate, and the partisan behavior of legislators when questions of state admission were debated and voted on had resulted in a striking pattern of straight party voting. This pattern spanned seven decades of American history, but it came to an end following the admission of Arizona and New Mexico in 1912. To the dynamic of two parties attempting to maximize their potential share of the Senate was added the growing sectional divide in the Democratic Party. Northern Democrats became strong advocates of state admission, supporting the admission of Republican territories in even greater numbers than the Republican Party did. Southern Democrats, by contrast, saw each additional member as a dilution of their power. To southern members of Congress, the admission of new states became a fundamental threat to their ability to maintain the caste controls and segregation that they saw as a core content of citizenship.

In summary, the issue-specific ideal points of the 85th and 86th Congresses clearly best explain the story of Alaska and Hawaii state admission. If we were to rely on aggregate estimates, we would not correctly identify the members who were pivotal to lawmaking in this area.

The Voting Rights Act of 1965

After ascending to the presidency upon the assassination of John F. Kennedy in 1964, Lyndon Johnson quickly guided to passage core elements of the Kennedy program, including a tax cut of 20 percent, the 1964 Civil Rights

---

[28]Trussell, "Hawaii Wins House Test on Statehood." It is worth noting that Republicans such as Richard Nixon rejected the linkage between the statehood debate and the investigations of Communist activity on the island.

Act, and the beginning of the War on Poverty (Matusow 1986, 131). The 1964 elections were a landslide victory for the president and the Democratic Party in Congress, with Johnson carrying all but Sen. Barry Goldwater's home state of Arizona and five states of the South. The electoral coalition assembled by Johnson was remarkably broad, including not only traditional Democratic constituencies and "a majority of white Protestants, suburbanites, and Midwest farmers," but active support from influential members of the corporate elite, all traditionally Republican constituencies (151). The scale of the Democratic victory made the administration significantly less reliant on the support of southern members. Of the 295 Democrats in the House, 196 were from outside the thirteen-state South, as were 44 of the 68 Democratic senators.

The 89th (1965–66) was a landmark Congress in terms of legislative productivity, in part because of its large Democratic majority. This Congress produced such notable legislation as the 1965 Voting Rights Act and Immigration and Nationality Act; established Medicare; introduced the U.S. government into education through the Elementary and Secondary School Act and the Higher Education Act; passed important international relations legislation, including the Food for Freedom Act; and voted on large and significant defense appropriations. The most important organization and scope bills considered were ones to establish a cabinet-level department for housing and urban development and to establish the Department of Transportation. This Congress was truly remarkable in the amount of landmark laws it passed. By all accounts, one of the most important of the laws passed by this Congress was the 1965 Voting Rights Act, which we explore in greater detail here.

Pressure for a voting rights bill was coming from both inside and outside the federal government, and it had been growing steadily throughout the early 1960s. The U.S. Commission on Civil Rights (1959, 135) provided institutional support to the claims of civil rights leaders that the existing legislation to secure the vote was insufficient, and the commission called for federal action, noting that "legislation presently on the books is inadequate to assure that all our qualified citizens shall enjoy the right to vote (135)." The civil rights movement stepped up efforts to register African Americans in January 1965, focusing especially on areas in the Black Belt of Alabama, and in early February President Johnson announced that he would seek new legislation on this matter.

From its inception, the bill, which was written in consultations between Attorney General Nicholas Katzenbach and Senate Minority Leader Everett Dirksen, was a bipartisan bill pursued with full cooperation between the administration and the Senate Republican leadership.[29] Johnson sent the bill to

---

[29]Nan Robertson, "Johnson Pressed for a Voting Law," *New York Times*, March 9, 1965, p. 24; E. W. Kenworthy, "Johnson to Address Congress Tonight on Vote Rights Bill," *New York Times*, March 15, 1965, p. 1.

Congress on March 17, 1965, two days after a speech in which he urged passage of the bill and embraced the rhetoric of the civil rights movement. At the core of the legislation was the establishment of a system of federal registrars, who would be sent to any state or political subdivision where less than 50 percent of the voting-age population was registered to vote or had voted in November 1964; and the suspension of literacy tests in the states covered (Alabama, Alaska, Georgia, Louisiana, Mississippi, and South Carolina). The states and subdivisions covered could not change their voting and registration procedures without approval from the attorney general or the U.S. District Court for the District of Columbia. The debates in Congress would center on whether there should be an automatic trigger or whether the attorney general should be empowered to appoint federal registrars upon receiving complaints and obtaining a determination of discrimination from a federal district court, and on whether the legislation should outlaw the poll tax on state and local elections.

The pivotal member, by all accounts, was the Republican from Illinois, Senator Dirksen. Not only did he help draft the legislation, but he was able to defeat efforts to prohibit local and state poll taxes by warning that he might not be able to get sufficient Republican support for cloture. More broadly, the legislation was only able to pass because there was a sufficiently large contingent of Republican senators who supported the legislation and who, on sovereignty policy, were situated around the filibuster pivot. But the positions of Republicans on sovereignty policy were not the same as their positions on all other votes, or even on domestic policy: had preferences been arrayed on this issue as they were on domestic policy, it is considerably less likely that the bill would have passed, since the filibuster members would have been primarily southern Democrats. Figure 4.9 provides smoothed histograms for the Senate for aggregate-level ideal points, domestic policies, and sovereignty issues. The sovereignty-specific estimates versus the aggregate scores for the Senate histogram show southerners to be much further apart and much more extreme than their northern Democrat colleagues. The sovereignty histogram provides a nice visual of how Republicans were clustered around the filibuster pivot.

Figure 4.10 provides a list of the pivotal members of the 89th Congress for the House and Senate, determined by aggregate scores as well by sovereignty scores. The Senate filibuster pivot is particularly informative (bottom of figure 4.10). The figure lists the pivotal members as the ten senators surrounding the sixty-seventh member opposite the president. The aggregate scores show that southern Democrats dominate this pivot. Six of the ten senators are southerners for the aggregate scores. In contrast, the sovereignty-specific scores show that nine of the ten senators are Republicans. Clearly, the sovereignty scores are more appropriate for understanding the politics of the Voting Rights Act than aggregate scores. In fact, we get the story completely wrong with the aggregate scores.

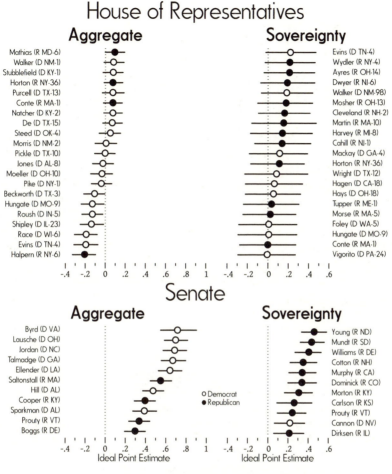

Figure 4.10
Pivotal Members, 89th Congress, 1965 to 1967

The most important controversy arising during the debate on this bill was whether the legislation should outlaw the use of the poll tax in state and local elections. This ban was opposed by not only the administration but the Senate leadership of both parties; Dirksen was especially adamant in insisting that the provision was of dubious constitutionality. He warned that the changes passed by the Senate Judiciary Committee threatened to "jeopardize the whole measure"[30] and that, "unless the poll-tax amendment was erased, he doubted

---

[30]Joseph Hearst, "Units of Both Houses Alter Vote Measure," *Chicago Tribune*, April 9, 1965, p. 23.

that Senate leaders could muster the two-thirds majority it would take to shut off a Southern filibuster."[31]

An offer by Dirksen and Senate Majority Leader Mike Mansfield of a bill that did not include the poll tax prohibition led to a showdown with the liberal bloc headed by Senator Edward Kennedy. The liberals were defeated by a vote of 45–49, with most northern Democrats supporting the prohibition and most southerners and Republicans in opposition. A week later a compromise was reached: the bill would include a congressional finding that the poll tax was used to deny the suffrage based on race and instructing the attorney general to seek a judicial decision on the matter. This measure was approved 69–20. The two votes on the poll tax allow us to see which members were pivotal in the Senate. We would expect the successfully passed amendment to reflect the positions of the pivotal members, and indeed, the switchers are considerably more concentrated around the median when arrayed using sovereignty rather than domestic or international relations estimates. This further suggests that issue-specific estimates provide greater leverage in identifying pivotal members.

The administration recognized that Dirksen was key to securing Republican support for a cloture vote: "You can't get cloture in the Senate," one White House aide announced, "without Dirksen working like hell for it" (MacNeil 1970, 258). After twenty-four days of debate, Dirksen was able to round up sufficient support for a cloture vote on May 25. Nine conservative Republicans voted against cloture, as well as most southerners. The next day the Senate passed the bill by a vote of 77–19, with all the nay votes coming from southern members.

The House committee had also included a poll tax prohibition, which House Republicans opposed and which they sought to remove through a substitute bill; that bill would fail when 21 Republicans and 40 southern Democrats voted against it. The eventual Republican defectors included both "liberals from urban areas" and "conservative Republicans who felt they could not be put in the position, either morally or politically, of voting for a bill less tough than the Administration measure."[32] The House passed the legislation 333–85, with 61 southern Democrats and 24 Republicans—8 of them from outside the South—voting against it.

The main difference between the two bills was the poll tax repeal passed by the House. Again, Senator Dirksen's opposition to including poll tax repeal in the bill was central to the outcome: "If the House conferees stood firm on the poll tax ban, Mr. Dirksen would probably wage an all-out fight against

---

[31] "Ban on Poll Tax Argued in Senate," *New York Times*, April 24, 1965, p. 12.

[32] E. W. Kenworthy, "GOP Voting Bill Falters in House," *New York Times*, July 9, 1965, p. 10.

accepting the conference report."[33] Ultimately, the House conferees conceded on the poll tax and approved the conference report 328–74; the Senate followed the next day with a vote of 79–18.

For its supporters, the voting rights bill was seen as reflecting core commitments of American citizenship, a central component of sovereignty. On beginning debate in the Senate, Dirksen laid out his belief that the denial of the franchise to African Americans violated not only the Fifteenth Amendment but foundational values of the American republic: "Is there consent of the governed when Negroes are taxed, compelled to render military service, subjected to criminal laws and required to pay for various services when they are barred from voting on such questions."[34] The president, in his address to Congress, likewise tied the bill to what he presented as core values of American citizenship.

The opponents of the legislation likewise framed their positions in terms of foundational commitments of American citizenship. There were some echoes of the defense of white supremacy that had marked earlier debates on civil rights: Senator Allen Ellender of Louisiana based his opposition on the fact that blacks outnumbered whites in a number of districts and allowing them to vote meant that "you could have governments of many towns and counties in this state in the hands of incompetents."[35] More frequently, southerners "rested their defense almost entirely on the right of the states, under Article 1, Section 2 of the Constitution, to determine their own qualifications for voting."[36] For both its supporters and detractors, the bill was seen as touching on core commitments of American citizenship.

---

[33] E. W. Kenworthy, "Senate Approves Voting Rights Bill in 77-to-19 Ballot," *New York Times*, May 27, 1965, p. 24.

[34] John Averill, "Senate Opens Debate on Voting Rights Bill," *Los Angeles Times*, April 23, 1965, p. 5.

[35] E. W. Kenworthy, "Congress Ready to Move Swiftly on Voting Rights," *New York Times*, March 17, 1965, p. 27.

[36] E. W. Kenworthy, "Senate, 70 to 30, Invokes Closure on Voting Rights," *New York Times*, May 26, 1965, p. 25. It is worth noting that while southerners opposed the bill and mounted a filibuster against it, by most accounts they did not put up as significant a fight as they did with previous civil rights legislation. Many southerners who opposed the 1964 bill suggested that they might be willing to vote for the Voting Rights Act, and several southerners did in fact vote yea. Senator J. William Fulbright of Arkansas, for instance, stated that "I am for the right of people to vote," and that "the probability is that I can support the bill" (Kenworthy, "Congress Ready to Move Swiftly"). The "endgame dynamic" identified by Alexander Keyssar (2009, 34) probably explains their relative restraint: "Parties that formerly resisted reform would drop their opposition, regardless of their convictions, because they did not want to risk antagonizing a new bloc of voters." This dynamic and the central role of voting in understandings of American citizenship were recognized by contemporaries; see John Averill, "Johnson's Plea for Vote Law," *Los Angeles Times*, March 16, 1965, p. 22.

It is not surprising that we find the pivotal legislator in the Senate, Senator Dirksen—who not only co-authored the bill with the attorney general but leveraged his importance to ensure sufficient Republican support to achieve cloture in order to shape the final legislation—within the pivotal filibuster zone when we array senators using sovereignty-specific ideal point estimates. When we compare the filibuster pivot, the members surrounding the sixty-seventh senator, using different issue-specific estimates, the pivotal members using sovereignty estimates are primarily Republicans, while the pivotal members using domestic estimates are primarily southern Democrats (see figure 4.10). Were we to use domestic-specific estimates, we would expect the southern members to have been pivotal, reducing the likelihood of a successful cloture vote. This is reflected in the legislative history: Republicans—and Dirksen in particular—were able to extract important concessions from liberals and secure administration support for many of their positions. The administration supported Dirksen on the poll tax and was "reluctant to offend Mr. Dirksen, whose help may be needed on other legislation and who commands the Republican votes needed for closure."[37] This should be compared with the failure to pass the 1966 civil rights bill, which died in the Senate when Dirksen chose to not press his members to support cloture. Dirksen opposed elements of the bill, which would have focused on discrimination in housing markets, as potentially unconstitutional. That his opposition was critical in the bill's defeat supports my claim that Dirksen was the pivotal member on sovereignty policy.[38]

CONCLUSION

This chapter has shown that policy issue substance is a critical component of any understanding of lawmaking. The fact that members clearly possess distinct preferences across policy issue areas is a topic separate from Poole and Rosenthal's work on the dimensionality of the political space. Working on multiple levels, I have demonstrated here what is lost in our study of policymaking when we exclude policy issue substance. At best, we can only partially understand lawmaking by treating the policy process as being similar across policy types. In some cases, the stakes involved might not seem to be that great, but in other cases we are left with an inaccurate picture of lawmaking. The good news is that simply measuring political preferences more accurately by focusing on policy issue substance enables us to better evaluate our current theoretical models of lawmaking without reinventing them.

[37] E. W. Kenworthy, "Senate Reaches Poll Tax Accord," *New York Times*, May 20, p. 29.
[38] E. W. Kenworthy, "Rights Bill Gains: House Unit Avoids Test on Housing," *New York Times*, June 17, 1966, p. 1.

APPENDIX

Table 4.A1 Probit Results

	Dependent Variable			
	Chinese Exclusion Act		**Espionage Act (Second Vote)**	
Ideal Point Estimate Used				
Aggregate	0.45***		−1.49***	
	(0.10)		(0.12)	
Sovereignty		−0.374*		−1.04***
		(0.199)		(0.09)
Constant	0.85***	0.89***	0.08	−0.02
	(0.10)	(0.10)	(0.09)	(0.08)
Observations	221	220	368	347
Correctly predicted	174	178	322	287
	(78.7%)	(80.9%)	(87.5%)	(82.7%)
Incorrectly predicted	47	42	46	60
	(21.3%)	(19.1%)	(12.5%)	(17.3%)

Notes: Standard errors in parentheses. Relevant votes were excluded when calculating ideal points. *** $p < 0.01$, ** $p < 0.05$, * $p < 0.1$

Chapter V

Legislative Accomplishment and Policy Issue Substance

AT THE CENTER OF THIS book is an ambitious empirical effort to better understand the importance of policy substance to lawmaking. Such an understanding requires that we have appropriate direct measures of actual lawmaking. Unfortunately, less is known (empirically) than should be about statute-making in the United States because we lack pre–World War II data and also because we possess few data that disaggregate lawmaking by policy issue area (Brady and Cooper 1981). In an attempt to remedy these problems, this chapter conceptualizes and constructs a comprehensive lawmaking data set that provides measures of legislative accomplishment in general as well as by policy issue area. This data set could significantly improve our understanding of lawmaking in the United States, as it helps to overcome an array of measurement-related problems that have plagued past researchers. Ultimately, it is a tool that provides a new and fresh approach to the study of lawmaking, not only in this book but in political science generally.

I begin by describing the type of data needed to better test current congressional-centered theories of lawmaking and provide an empirical spine to some important questions that are central to American political development. After presenting the case for direct measures of legislative accomplishment based on actual lawmaking data to supplement roll call–based measures of legislative behavior, I follow up by providing a detailed account of the conceptualization and estimation of legislative significance for my lawmaking data. The next section serves as a hinge between the individual significance estimates for specific laws and a macro-level measure of legislative accomplishment by explaining the construction of Congress-by-Congress measures of legislative accomplishment, including measures broken down by the policy-coding schema. I close the chapter by explaining how to merge the policy issue substance data constructed in chapter 2 with the significance lawmaking data introduced here.

NEEDED: DIRECT MEASURES OF LEGISLATIVE ACCOMPLISHMENT

The study of lawmaking—by which is meant the enactment of public statutes— in the United States has a long and important history in political science. One very important characteristic of much of the literature that analyzes Congress and lawmaking is the reliance of the bulk of its empirical investigations on roll call measures (for example, interest group scores, ideal point estimates, roll rates, coalition sizes, or voting behavior on selected votes) instead of lawmaking data. In other words, a behavior-based measure is often used as a proxy for actual lawmaking.

Clearly roll calls and lawmaking are related, but this relationship is not fully or even well understood. What is known about roll call voting makes it very plausible that such data may pose theoretical and econometric problems for studying the statute-making process, even though they are clearly excellent data for measuring political behavior in Congress. Nonetheless, the Congress literature includes many prominent examples of the substitution of roll call voting data for lawmaking data. For example, on the basis of roll calls alone, Keith Poole and Howard Rosenthal (1997, 58, emphasis added) write:

> As a result of the "tyranny of the majority," slight changes in mean position [of NOMINATE scores] when accompanied by a shift in majority control, can lead to *substantial changes in policy....* We find that the swings in policy during the nineteenth and the early twentieth century were much greater than those later in the twentieth century. Although the New Deal initiated a large policy shift comparable to those of the nineteenth century, since the end of World War II, policy swings have dampened considerably.

More recently, Gary Cox and Matthew McCubbins (2005, 51) have explained that, "in order to test our main points—that the Reed rules permanently significantly changed voting behavior and *policy outcomes* in the House... we employ a dataset of House final passage votes." Although it is certainly true that the direction of policy change can be determined from final passage votes, the generalizability and interpretation of inferences on lawmaking based on roll calls is unclear. Without knowing why some votes are recorded whereas others are not, it is unclear what to make of inferences from the nonrandom subset that does.

Assessments of lawmaking using roll calls *depend critically on the assumption that roll call behavior parallels lawmaking behavior.*[1] Collaborative work

---

[1] Several other prominent scholars have questioned the use of roll calls to study all congressional behavior. For example, Richard Hall (1996, 2) argues: "Floor voting is only one and probably not the most important form of participation in the legislative process. Building a coalition

that I have conducted with Josh Clinton demonstrates that this assumption is not fully justified (Clinton and Lapinski 2008).

In this collaborative work, we empirically find that policy issue content, legislative significance, and political context matter profoundly for whether a public statute receives a roll call vote. Although I do not summarize all of the findings here (for the specific details, see Clinton and Lapinski 2008), it is the case that substituting roll calls for public laws is probably only appropriate for the most salient, landmark legislation. Of course, this is a good finding for those who use roll calls to study lawmaking: Congress scholars are clearly most interested in studying important laws. However, it is also the case that there are large differences in the rates at which roll call votes can be observed across policy issue areas. Although my findings are far from definitive, they do show clearly that it would be unwise to not attempt to create direct measures of legislative performance to study lawmaking. Roll call–based measures have many uses for studying Congress, but there is much we do not know about them. Better to have a direct measure of legislative performance rather than only a proxy. The next section begins to introduce such a direct measure to study lawmaking.

MEASURING LEGISLATIVE SIGNIFICANCE

To better understand lawmaking, especially how it varies by policy issue substance area, appropriate data on lawmaking and legislative accomplishment must be constructed.[2] The data ideally should possess at least four characteristics: they must be based on actual legislation; they must span a long time horizon so that they are relevant for the study of American political development; they must separate trivial from important legislation; and they must be broken down by theoretically relevant policy issue areas. In order to construct the data that meet these criteria, it is useful to draw on the contributions of other scholars who have expanded our knowledge about lawmaking. For example, previous work has shown that Congress passes thousands of inconsequential laws, a point made by Charles Cameron (2000, 37): "There is a little secret about Congress that is never discussed in the legions of textbooks

---

for a legislative package, drafting particular amendments, planning and executing parliamentary strategy, bargaining with or persuading colleagues to adopt one's point of view—all these activities weigh more heavily than voting in the decision-making calculus of most bills." Likewise, Peter van Doren (1990, 332) argues that "the main problem with roll call studies [is] the nonrandom nature of roll calls themselves. Roll call votes occur only if policy proposals receive committee approval and do not languish on the calendar and enough members desire a roll call vote" (see also Van Doren 1991). This argument is based on his examination of atomic energy and coal policy in the House from 1947 to 1976.

[2] This section is adapted from Clinton and Lapinski (2006).

on American government: the vast bulk of legislation produced by that august body is stunningly banal. The president, like almost everyone else, couldn't care less about them." Should theories of lawmaking be tested on such trivial legislation? If one believes that the nature of the politics probably depends on the stakes of the policy being considered (which appears reasonable), then the answer is clearly no. To separate the trivial from the consequential, it is necessary to distinguish legislative significance.[3] In other words, we need to determine the importance of every law. Measuring legislative significance is also important because the information it provides can ultimately be used to construct direct measures of legislative accomplishment broken down by substantive issue areas. How can legislative significance best be measured across time?

The first decision made for this study was to characterize every enactment that Congress passed over a long time period. This effort resulted in the collection of a comprehensive data set of the 37,766 public statutes passed between the years 1877 and 1994 (the 45th to 103rd Congresses).[4] Every one of these statutes has an estimated statute-level significance score. These statute-level estimates for every enactment contrast with existing measures that treat all significant and insignificant legislation as equally important and perfectly measured—an idea explained in the next section.

Significant Legislation and the Role of "Raters"

This work takes as its substantive foundation the pioneering work of David Mayhew. In his *Divided We Govern* (1991), Mayhew tackles the difficult issues of measurement and selection in an analysis of lawmaking and an assessment of the role of Congress and the president in the policymaking process. His analysis, which focuses directly on lawmaking rather than on indirect measures such as roll call votes, has provided important information and ideas about measuring the legislative accomplishment of Congress. Mayhew has increased our understanding of the type of data that are important for studying lawmaking; improved our definitions of "important," "notable," and "significant" legislation; and shown us the importance of testing theory and hypotheses against actual policy outputs. Of these three contributions, however, the second is the most opaque.

---

[3] Passing inconsequential laws is an important activity for members of Congress because such laws represent pork politics. In other words, such enactments are usually constituency-oriented. Pork barrel laws, of course, need not be insignificant. Often large omnibus bills are full of pork; see, for example, John Ferejohn's (1974) seminal study on pork politics, which focuses on highly significant rivers and harbors legislation between 1947 and 1968.

[4] Data collection is currently under way to update the significance data through the 111th Congress.

Although existing lists of legislation purport to identify legislation that is "landmark," "significant," "innovative," or "consequential," what is meant by "important" legislation is inevitably, if not hopelessly, imprecise. Any characteristics that could plausibly identify legislation as "defining" or "significant" are themselves plagued by imprecision. For example, Mayhew (1991, 37) defines important legislation as that which is "both innovative and consequential—or if viewed from the time of passage, thought likely to be consequential." What does he mean by "consequential" and "innovative"? Should policy innovation be measured by the percentage of the U.S. code that is changed by a statute or by how far a policy moves the status quo? Does "consequential" refer to the extent to which a policy changes existing laws, the number of people affected by the legislation, or the extent of that impact on the affected people? Even if a precise definition were possible, it would be impossibly complex to operationalize it. For example, although the Civil Rights Act of 1964 and the Voting Rights Act of 1965 are unquestionably two of the most consequential civil rights policies ever enacted in the United States, how do we assess the consequence and innovation of symbolic legislation such as the act that established Martin Luther King Day as a national holiday or the 1989 Flag Protection Act, which outlaws flag burning?[5]

Mayhew (1991, 40) utilizes both contemporaneous and retrospective evaluations of the policymaking process—essentially elite evaluations—to assess which legislative enactments meet this standard and qualify as "important."[6] The resulting list has strong validity and can be rationalized ex post, but there is no necessary relationship between the posited criteria of innovation and consequence and whether a statute is sufficiently noteworthy to appear in a review of the legislative session by major newspapers or in a policy history. Although innovative and consequential legislation is likely to be mentioned (and therefore captured by the measure), Mayhew admits that coverage of an enactment may also be affected by other characteristics, such as the level of controversy with which it is associated. Certainly legislation that fundamentally changes the nature of government would be controversial, but controversy may also stem from the political environment rather than the enactment itself. It is not implausible that identical legislation might result in substantially different levels

---

[5]Not only can symbols be very important to people, but by their very nature they are likely to be controversial and to capture the attention of the media and the public. Most observers would agree that allowing or prohibiting flag burning does not affect the day-to-day lives of as many Americans as the Civil Rights Act does, but deciding how to evaluate the comparative consequences of such enactments is not so clear.

[6]Enactments for Mayhew include constitutional amendments and Senate ratification of treaties but exclude "congressional resolutions, appropriations acts, very-short-term measures (such as a one-year extension of rent control in 1947), statutory amendments taken by themselves, and extensions or re-authorization acts that [seem] to offer little new."

of controversy, depending on the political environment. Legislation perceived as controversial during an era of political acrimony might pass with bipartisan support at a time of relative calm. Consequently, Mayhew's operationalization of importance—using notable legislation—effectively identifies three types of legislation: legislation controversial enough to warrant coverage; legislation with a great enough impact to warrant coverage; and legislation innovative enough to warrant coverage.

Attempts to specify the precise conditions under which a statute might be considered significant lead quickly to a list of conditions that prove difficult, if not impossible, to operationalize. Even if it were possible to specify precisely what constitutes an "important" statute, the usefulness of such an exercise is doubtful given how unlikely it is that a determination based on such standards could be made. The difficulty, if not futility, of such an exercise leads to a definition of significant legislation based explicitly on that which is notable. Consequently, the working definition of significant legislation here is a statute or constitutional amendment that has been identified as noteworthy by a reputable chronicler-rater of the congressional session.[7] This definition is identical to the one put forth by Mayhew in *Divided We Govern*. Although this measure is more accurately described as a way to identify notable legislation, the path followed here is to abide by the usage of others, like Mayhew, and to refer to "notable" legislation as "significant" legislation.

Following Mayhew (1991), I characterize raters according to whether their assessments are primarily contemporaneous or retrospective. Contemporaneous raters assess legislation at or near the time of enactment. Retrospective raters rely on hindsight to determine the noteworthiness of legislation in the context of both prior and subsequent events.

The Rater Data

The technique I use to code the rater data is identical to the method employed by Mayhew (1991). For each of the 37,766 laws in the data set, a team of researchers, including myself, identified mentions of legislation by the raters selected for this study. Specifically, all mentions of public enactments and policy changes were recorded and coded for content. One tricky issue was how to deal with mentions by raters who did not provide the exact wording or title of the legislation being mentioned. If the title of the statute was not present in the text, we searched through the index of the "History of Bills and Resolutions" in the *Congressional Record* and the index of the *Public Statutes at Large* to locate the bill in question. All mentioned bills received a dichotomous

---

[7]Note that Mayhew (1991) sometimes substitutes the word "notable" for "significant."

coding. A mentioned bill received a coding of 1, which meant "significant," or 0, which meant "not mentioned" and therefore "not significant."[8]

Separating the rater data into Mayhew's two categories, we begin with the *contemporaneous* rater data collected. Mayhew's sweep 1 draws on contemporaneous sources to construct a list of important enactments and constitutes the first rater used here. Another contemporaneous source is Baumgartner and Jones's Policy Agendas Project (2002, 2004), which collects information on every public statute enacted since 1948. Baumgartner and Jones's list of important enactments is based on the number of column lines devoted to each enactment in the *Congressional Quarterly Almanac (CQ)*.

Additional sources of contemporaneous assessments are the *New York Times* and the *Washington Post*. These measures were initially collected and summarized by Mayhew (1991) to form his sweep 1 assessment; subsequently, they were independently collected by Cameron (2000) and William Howell and his colleagues (2000). The latter combine information collected from these two newspapers with story coverage in *CQ* and Mayhew's series to construct a four-category ordinal measure of significance for the period from 1948 to 1993. Here I use an indicator of whether the legislation passes the lowest threshold for nontrivial legislation (A through C in the coding of Howell et al. 2000).[9]

Also used are the assessments made in the legislative wrap-ups of the *American Political Science Review (APSR)* and *Political Science Quarterly (PSQ)*. These journals summarized the year's proceedings in Congress for the years 1889 to 1925 (*PSQ*) and 1919 to 1948 (*APSR*).[10] Finally, we have used Eric Peterson's (2001) attempt to replicate Mayhew's coding technique for 1881 to 1945 by relying on contemporaneous sources that vary from Congress to Congress.

Retrospective rater data, the second type of rating data employed by Mayhew, are used here as well. Mayhew's sweep 2 for the 1948 to 1994 period and Peterson's (2001) replication of Mayhew's sweep 2 for the 1881 to 1947 period are two sources of retrospective ratings. In addition to the retrospective ratings of Mayhew and Peterson, which aggregate the determinations of

---

[8] The rater data are dichotomous, though information was collected on whether individual raters mentioned a bill more than once. For a more detailed discussion of this point, see Clinton and Lapinski (2006).

[9] A rating of C or above means that a given enactment is mentioned in the *Congressional Quarterly Almanac*, the *New York Times*, or the *Washington Post*. Although the higher thresholds of Howell et al. (2000) could be used, Baumgartner and Jones's (2002, 2004) measure already essentially accounts for this information.

[10] Although the *Western Political Quarterly (WPQ)* continued the legislative wrap-ups after the *APSR* stopped—even using the same author (Floyd Riddick) used by the *APSR* for a number of Congresses—the content of *WPQ* changed significantly, making these wrap-ups uninformative for the purposes of this study.

several divergent policy histories, I also use several general political history and policymaking series, including the eleven period-specific volumes of the New American Nation Series—a "comprehensive, cooperative history of the area now embraced in the United States, from the days of discovery to the present" (Matusow 1986, ix)—and the American Presidency Series.[11] In the American Presidency Series, "each book treats the then-current problems facing the United States and its people and how the president and his associates felt about, thought about, and worked to cope with these problems. In short, the authors in this series strive to recount and evaluate the record of each administration and to identify its distinctiveness and relationships to the past, its own time, and the future" (Greene 2000, ix).[12]

Additional sources of retrospective ratings include: Lawrence Chamberlain's *The President, Congress, and Legislation* (1946), which contains a detailed history of U.S. policymaking across ten distinct spheres; John Reynolds's "Divided We Govern: Research Note" (1995), a "mini-research report" that culled the *Enduring Vision* textbook for mentions of important legislation between 1877 and 1948 to test for the effect of divided government on policymaking before World War II; Irving Sloan's *American Landmark Legislation* (1984), a compilation of a selective list of laws based on the

---

[11] The New American Nation Series includes: Arthur S. Link's *Woodrow Wilson and the Progressive Era, 1910—1917* (1954), George E. Mowry's *The Era of Theodore Roosevelt, 1900-1912* (1958), Harold U. Faulkner's *Politics, Reform, and Expansion, 1890-1900* (1959), Eric F. Goldman's *The Crucial Decade and After: America, 1945-1960* (1960), John D. Hick's *Republican Ascendancy, 1921-1933* (1960), William E. Leuchtenburg's *Franklin D. Roosevelt and the New Deal, 1932-1940* (1963), Russell A. Buchanan's *The United States and World War II*, vols. 1 and 2 (1964), John A. Garratty's *The New Commonwealth, 1877-1890* (1968), Allen J. Matusow's *The Unraveling of America: A History of Liberalism in the 1960s* (1986), and Robert H. Ferrell's *Woodrow Wilson and World War I, 1917-1921* (1985). Although Vaughn Davis Bornet's *The American Presidency of Lyndon B. Johnson* (1983) is a part of the American Presidency Series, it differs substantially in its treatment of legislation. Consequently, it was treated as a separate rater.

[12] The American Presidency Series includes Paolo E. Coletta's *The Presidency of William Howard Taft* (1973), Eugene P. Trani and David L. Wilson's *The Presidency of Warren G. Harding* (1977), Lewis L. Gould's *The Presidency of William McKinley* (1980) and *The Presidency of Theodore Roosevelt* (1991), Justus D. Doenecke's *The Presidencies of James A. Garfield and Chester A. Arthur* (1981), Donald R. McCoy's *The Presidency of Harry S. Truman* (1984), Martin L. Fausold's *The Presidency of Herbert C. Hoover* (1985), Homer B. Socolofsky and Allan B. Spetter's *The Presidency of Benjamin Harrison* (1987), Ari Hoogenboom's *The Presidency of Rutherford B. Hayes* (1988), Richard E. Welch Jr.'s *The Presidencies of Grover Cleveland* (1988), Chester J. Pach Jr. and Elmo Richardson's *The Presidency of Dwight D. Eisenhower* (1991), James N. Giglio's *The Presidency of John F. Kennedy* (1991), Burton I. Kaufman's *The Presidency of James Earl Carter Jr.* (1993), Kendrick A. Clements's *The Presidency of Woodrow Wilson* (1992), John Robert Greene's *The Presidency of Gerald R. Ford* (1995) and *The Presidency of George Bush* (2000), Robert H. Ferrell's *The Presidency of Calvin Coolidge* (1998), Melvin Small's *The Presidency of Richard Nixon* (1999), and George T. McJimsey's *The Presidency of Franklin Delano Roosevelt* (2000). This series is supplemented by Michael Schaller's *Reckoning with Reagan: American and Its President in the 1980s* (1992).

"important national significance they had at the time Congress passed them" and their lasting effect on "one dimension or another of American life"; Paul Light's *Government's Greatest Achievements: From Civil Rights to Homeland Defense* (2002); and several of the history books on public affairs that are identified in Mayhew's *America's Congress* (2000), which we treat as separate raters. Two final retrospective raters come from the work of the Congressional Research Service. Christopher Dell and Stephen Stathis (1982) chronicle congressional effort from 1789 (1st Congress) to 1980 (96th Congress), and Stathis's recent solo work, *Landmark Legislation 1774–2002* (2003), expands and extends but does not strictly restate the assessments of Dell and Stathis (1982). Table 5.1 summarizes the raters, including the number of statutes covered and the number of statutes mentioned. Statutes passed during the time period but not mentioned by a rater are counted as unmentioned.

Because we cannot identify precisely how the legislation mentioned by raters corresponds to some acceptable definition of policy significance, constructing the "best" measure would seem to be impossible. Consider the task of resolving the differences between the lists compiled by Mayhew (1991) and Stathis (2003) for statutes passed in 1981. Mayhew identifies only two important statutes: the Economic Recovery Tax Act (PL 97-34) and the Omnibus Budget Reconciliation Act (PL 97-35). Stathis mentions these and adds the Veterans' Health Care, Training, and Small Business Loan Act (PL 97-72), Restrictions on Military Assistance and Sales to El Salvador (PL 97-113), Fiscal 1982 Department of Defense Appropriations (PL 97-114), and the Social Security Act Amendments (PL 97-123). Are we to conclude that two significant statutes were enacted in 1981, or six? Or some intermediate number? The justification for choosing any of these numbers is unclear. Are the Social Security Act Amendments important for having restored the minimum benefit eliminated by the Omnibus Budget Reconciliation Act and enabling the Old-Age and Survivors Insurance fund to borrow from the Hospital Insurance and Disability Insurance trust funds? Is it important or unimportant that the Veterans' Health Care, Training, and Small Business Loan Act extended GI Bill eligibility for Vietnam veterans by two years? It is difficult to resolve such differences because the basis for these distinctions is unclear. The previous example explains why a statistical model is needed to adjudicate this type of problem.

A benefit of using a statistical method to leverage the rater data collected for every public statute in the data set is that it permits the data to determine the appropriate resolution. Relationships between raters determine the relative contribution of each rater to the composite significance estimate. Because the raters employed are those who explicitly or implicitly identify significant legislation, the resulting list is likely to consist of "high-stakes" legislation on "important," "innovative," or "consequential" policy. Despite this

Table 5.1 Summary of Raters

Rater	Type	Time Period	Enactments	
			Rated	Mentioned
Mayhew (1991), sweep 1 (including updates)	C	80th–103rd	16,933	216
Baumgartner and Jones (2002, 2004)	C	81st–103rd	16,026	550
Howell et al. (2000)	C	79th–103rd	17,667	2282
American Political Science Review	C	66th–80th	11,893	483
Political Science Quarterly	C	50th–68th	9,935	286
Peterson (2001), sweep 1	C	47th–79th	20,220	213
Mayhew (1991), sweep 2 including updates)				
	R	80th–101st	15,878	197
Peterson (2001), sweep 2	R	47th–79th	20,220	144
New American Nation Series	R	45th–90th	29,802	340
American Presidency Series	R	45th–88th; 91st–102nd	35,371	674
Chamberlain (1946)	R	45th–76th	18,682	105
Reynolds (1995)	R	45th–80th	21,741	84
Sloan (1984)	R	45th–80th	21,741	16
Light (2002)	R	81st–103rd	16,026	164
Grantham (1987)	R	81st–99th	13,608	126
Barone (1990)	R	81st–100th	14,321	63
Blum (1991)	R	87th–93rd	4,954	30
Dell and Stathis (1982)	R	45th–96th	33,589	582
Stathis (2003)	R	45th–103rd	37,767	739

ambiguity, for purposes of exposition, the estimates are referred to as measuring "significance."[13]

The number of available raters and the differences evident in their ratings raise three additional questions that are largely avoided in the literature

---

[13] Existing measures are most properly conceived as lists that reflect the raters' judgments as to which statutes are most deserving of mention in their chronicle of legislative activity. Although legislation is presumably notable because it is "consequential," "influential," or "novel," this is not necessarily the case. Several of the raters explicitly claim to identify consequential legislation, but nothing ensures either that all consequential legislation is mentioned or that inconsequential legislation is unmentioned.

on measuring legislative significance. How should rater disagreement be interpreted? How should such heterogeneity affect a measure of significance? And how can the assessments of raters of different time periods be compared?

There are three ways to interpret rater heterogeneity. First, raters may differ because they use different criteria. For example, it may be that the American Presidency Series focuses on legislation related to presidential programs and the New American Nation Series focuses on statutes that are retrospectively notable and "stand the test of time." If this is the case, then a composite measure is problematic—the aggregate measure that reflects disparate concerns is less meaningful than the individual ratings. Raters were consciously selected to minimize this possibility; the selected raters explicitly seek to identify significant legislation or identify the major legislative events of the time period. Furthermore, the statistical model can test whether rater assessments are based on different underlying dimensions.

Second, raters may employ the same criteria but different thresholds for designating statutes as significant. For example, in its annual wrap-up, the *American Political Science Review* may be more likely to identify a statute as constituting an important policy change than a rater such as Sloan, who surveys the entire time period before making such an identification. In other words, two raters may agree about the dimension of interest but differ on the threshold that defines significance. Contemporaneous assessments are most vulnerable to this possibility, because the publication of annual reviews may result in inflated assessments during periods of relative inactivity. Finally, raters may make mistakes in their assessments. The process of culling through and assessing legislation is exhausting and time-consuming. Raters may miss legislation that would have qualified as noteworthy according to their own standards.

The literature takes two approaches to rater disagreement. Some argue that one list is preferable to another (see, for example, Howell et al. 2000; Kelly 1993; Mayhew 1993). Although such comparisons raise important points, it is difficult to assess them objectively and conclusively in light of the difficulties already noted in determining the relationship between any measure of significance and a statute's "true" significance. Researchers also use competing lists in order to ignore the measurement debates and instead determine whether the results of interest depend on the list of significant legislation. In other words, they replicate their analyses using different measures (see, for example, Coleman 1999; Krehbiel 1998). Although pervasive, this approach fails to account for rater heterogeneity and examines only whether coefficients of interest, for example, depend on the measure used.

Accounting for rater heterogeneity and unanimity is important because it conveys information about both the magnitude and the certainty of this assessment of legislative significance. It makes little sense to treat the twelve statutes that receive unanimous mention by active raters equivalently to the 2,164 statutes mentioned by a single rater between 1877 and 1994. Rater agreement may indicate increased significance or increased certainty about the probability that the legislation is significant relative to the significance of a bill that experiences rater disagreement.

Two additional concerns plague existing lists. First, the classification of landmark legislation is extremely coarse. It is hard to believe that the Voting Rights Act of 1982 and the Voting Rights Act of 1965 are equally significant. However, that is the conclusion suggested by the dichotomous ratings of Stathis (2003) and Mayhew (1991). Second, existing measures fail to quantify the precision of the measures. Rater disagreement suggests that our assessments of legislative significance are uncertain. Although we may be quite confident of the importance of the Civil Rights Act of 1964, which is mentioned by each of the twelve raters covering the period, we may be less certain of the significance of a statute mentioned by only two of the twelve raters. It is implausible that we are equally certain of the significance of the Civil Rights Act of 1964 and public law 379, which passed the same year and established water resource research centers at land-grant colleges and state universities.

A final difficulty results from over-time comparisons. Because not every rater evaluates every statute, it is difficult to know how to compare ratings from different eras. For example, Peterson (2001) attempts to extend Mayhew's (1991) sweep 1 and sweep 2 ratings to an earlier era. However, because Peterson and Mayhew use different sources and never rate a common set of statutes, it is impossible to determine whether they employ the same significance threshold and consequently how the two periods compare in terms of the number of significant enactments. It is also impossible to compare legislative productivity and to test theories of lawmaking using legislative output both before and after World War II unless one uses one of the few lists that extend across time (for example, Stathis 2003).

The Statistical Model of Legislative Significance

To account for the information contained in all of the various ratings and recover a more fine-grained measure of legislative significance along with standard errors, I use an item-response model. This statistical technique provides a means of leveraging all available information, facilitating over-time comparisons and testing some underlying assumptions (for example, that all raters' assessments are determined by a common latent dimension). After introducing this statistical model, which also provides a means of integrating the rater data described in this section with statute characteristics that may be correlated with the statute's importance, I discuss the statistical model employed to estimate statute-level significance scores that draw on all of the rater data as well as data collected on bill-level characteristics (for a complete description of the model, see Clinton and Lapinski 2006).

The item-response model was developed for and is widely used in educational testing research, but it can be used to integrate other data as well.
In the case of the significance scores, data about the characteristics of every
public statute in the data set ($N = 37,766$) are included in the estimate of
significance. It is important to understand the model's basic intuition. The
item-response model is commonly used in educational testing because it
models how "items"—commonly, questions on a test—discriminate between
individuals on the basis of a latent trait such as ability, aptitude, or intelligence.
In other words, the item-response model is a model of how observable
responses reflect an underlying latent dimension. The model is specifically
designed to address the complication of the parameters of interest that are
unobserved: the latent ability of the test-takers and the ability of the test
questions to discriminate between test-takers. In applying the models, previous
work in political science has recognized the similarities between students who
are answering questions and legislators (or judges) who are casting votes (see,
for example, Clinton, Jackman and Rivers 2004; Martin and Quinn 2002).
Poole and Rosenthal's (1997) seminal work on ideal point estimation uses a
very similar model. Applications of this model exploit a natural comparison
between students being rated by examiners and statutes being assessed by
congressional chroniclers.

To estimate the significance of every public statute passed by Congress, the
item-response model draws on the comprehensive data set described earlier.
The data set consists of each of the 37,766 public statutes passed between
1877 and 1994 (45th to 103rd Congresses). This data set includes information
on every public statute enacted during this period, including a large sample
(twenty) of elite evaluations of the importance of public enactments at different
points in time as well as a number of other measures by which the importance
of a bill can be ascertained: the amount of *Congressional Record* coverage, the
number of substitute bills, the session in which it was passed, whether a conference committee was required, and whether the statute was an omnibus bill.

The nonrater data were extremely time-consuming to collect: a coder
looked up each public enactment in the "History of Bills and Resolutions" in
the *Congressional Record* and then recorded and entered this information into
our database. The most difficult element to collect was the number of pages
in the *Congressional Record* dedicated to deliberating the bill. Each page in the
index had to be hand-counted and summed. The importance of the data on
bill characteristics cannot be understated, as the vast majority of legislation
is not mentioned as being significant by even a single rater. The importance
of discriminating among the nonrated legislation is discussed later in this
chapter.

The data are used to estimate a significance "score" for every public
enactment as well as a standard error. This is a very important contribution—
no other measure of legislative significance estimates standard errors—because

it helps us gauge the uncertainty associated with measuring legislative significance. This is accomplished by using a statistical model—the item-response model—to integrate all rater information and account for rater differences, as well as by leveraging data collected on the statutes themselves. As previously stated, the method reconciles disagreements and combines raters who assess different periods of American history to yield time-consistent significance estimates. This is a very important point because the model accounts for the fact that raters use different thresholds for determining significance (an idea elaborated upon in the appendix to this chapter). The statute-level estimates for every enactment also stand in contrast to existing measures that treat all legislation as equally significant and perfectly measured. These estimates discriminate between rated enactments, and to extend the ratings to statutes unmentioned by our raters, we use information regarding the amount of attention that Congress devoted to each statute, the number of substitute bills, whether a conference committee was required, and the session in which the legislation was introduced. In the next section, I discuss the individual-level statute estimates in slightly more detail.

Statute-Level Estimates

Of most interest to the study of lawmaking are the estimates and standard errors of legislative significance z for the 37,766 laws analyzed. Three estimates were computed in Clinton and Lapinski (2006): the mean rating, the item-response estimator described earlier in this chapter, and the integrated estimator that incorporates the bill characteristics data (for details of the estimates, see Clinton and Lapinski 2006). I use the integrated estimator in this book. This estimator uses the regression structure to distinguish between legislative enactments with identical mean ratings. This is most apparent in the unmentioned legislation. Whereas the normal item-response estimator locates all unmentioned statutes around 0, the inclusion of statute characteristics allows the significance of unrated legislative enactments to be distinguished. This is very important, as it allows me to distinguish among less significant legislation.

Table 5.2 provides an example of the power and face validity of these estimates for seven civil rights bills drawn from the list of public laws. Although examining the issue of civil rights is limiting in that most such legislating took place from the 1950s onward, it is an illustrative example given its long and important history in this country and the fact that many are familiar with it.

The highest score for a civil rights enactment, not surprisingly, is accorded to the Civil Rights Act of 1964. This bill massively expanded federal power over voting rights, outlawed discrimination in federally funded projects, and gave the attorney general new powers to prosecute state and local authorities who

Table 5.2 Examples of Civil Rights Enactments

Title	Congress	Estimate	Standard Error
Civil Rights Act of 1964	88th (HR 7152, PL 352)	1.86	0.428
Voting Rights Act of 1965	89th (S 1564, PL 110)	1.516	0.328
Voting Rights Act Amendments of 1982	97th (HR 3112, PL 205)	1.184	0.284
Civil Rights Act of 1957	85th (HR 6127, PL 315)	1.102	0.254
Civil Rights Act of 1960	86th (HR 8601, PL 449)	1.039	0.232
Civil Rights Commission extension	90th (HR 10805, PL 198)	0.145	0.36
Relief of Mrs. Elizabeth G. Mason and Civil Rights Commission extension	88th (HR 3369, PL 152)	1.491	0.598

did not desegregate public accommodations. This bill was truly a landmark achievement, and it deserves a place atop this list of civil rights legislation. The second-highest-scoring civil rights bill on this list is the Voting Rights Act of 1965. Building on the 1964 act, this enactment made it illegal to use literacy tests and voter qualifications to screen out voters, brought in federal examiners to supervise registration in states where such requirements had existed, and established criminal penalties for those who violated the act. Below these two very influential landmark laws fall three important enactments passed in 1957, 1960, and 1982. The 1982 enactment, passed during the presidency of Ronald Reagan, was popularly called the Voting Rights Act Amendment of 1982. This law extended the key components of the Voting Rights Act of 1965 for twenty-five years and gave private parties standing in federal court to sue to overturn any law or procedure resulting in de facto discrimination. The Civil Rights Act of 1957, marshaled by then-senator Lyndon B. Johnson, was a major enactment, but historical accounts show that the act that became law had been very much watered down. Still, it was the first act of its kind in nearly a century, and therefore even a diluted enactment is important. Quite near the 1957 act in terms of significance is the 1960 Civil Rights Act. This act gave federal judges the authority to assist people in voting and established criminal penalties for attempting to obstruct voting through violence.

Two other enactments are less significant when compared with these five enactments. Public law 90-198, which passed in 1967, extended the life of the Civil Rights Commission by three years and made a nontrivial appropriation of $2.65 million to support it. Clearly this enactment, though important, is qualitatively different from major legislation such as the 1964 and 1965 acts. The second of these lesser enactments, public law 88-152, received a score well below the other laws cited in the table. This law is a one-sentence amendment that extended the Civil Rights Commission for one year without an appropriation and is attached to what appears to be a private relief bill (for Mrs. Elizabeth Mason, whose husband died in combat in Belgium during World War II).

These seven enactments provide strong face validity to the measure. The scores associated with these enactments are sensible and provide considerable information about their relative importance. The measures account for the difference between the 1964 and 1965 enactments and the acts passed in 1957, 1960, and 1982. In contrast, most existing lists treat all of these enactments as identically "notable" or "significant."

The face validity of this measure is further established by its application to policies in housing and urban development. Given the late entry of the national government into housing and urban development issues, it is not surprising that three New Deal–era bills that essentially mark the government's entry into this arena rank very high in significance. The highest score for an enactment related to housing is accorded to the U.S. Housing Act of 1937, which created the United States Housing Authority (later the Public Housing Administration). This bill committed the federal government to providing financial assistance in the form of loans, contributions, and capital grants to the states and their public housing agencies for the construction of public housing for low-income families and the concomitant demolition of "unsafe and unsanitary" houses.

Another high-scoring bill is the 1934 National Housing Act, which established the Federal Housing Administration (FHA) and empowered it to insure financial institutions against any losses they might sustain as a result of making loans or advances of credits for the purpose of financing alterations, repairs, or improvements on real property. The bill also provided for a system of mutual mortgage insurance, the establishment of national mortgage associations, and the Federal Savings and Loan Insurance Corporation (FSLIC), which absorbed some of the risk from depositors. It greatly enhanced the affordability of mortgages and encouraged the construction of new homes and homeownership. Table 5.3 lists ten enactments across a range of significance scores within this policy area.

The Housing Act of 1961—also considered landmark legislation—provided federal funds for the first time for public transportation and the preservation of open land, created a new program of low-interest loans for families excluded from the public housing programs, funded the redevelopment of homes in areas marked for urban renewal projects, and provided and secured additional funds, as well as expanded authorization, for existing programs such as mortgage insurance, college housing, and subsidized housing costs for moderate- and low-income families. The Home Owners' Loan Act of 1933 created the Home Owners' Loan Corporation and empowered it to provide

Table 5.3 Examples of Housing and Urban Development Enactments

Title	Congress	Estimate	Standard Error
U.S. Housing Act of 1937	75th (S 1685, PL 412)	1.684	0.3346
National Housing Act of 1934	73rd (HR 9620, PL 479)	1.524	0.3289
Housing Act of 1961	87th (S 1922, PL 70)	1.418	0.2856
Home Owners' Loan Act of 1933	73rd (HR 5240, PL 43)	1.29	0.273
Housing Act of 1954	83rd (HR 7839, PL 560)	0.8011	0.2133
Housing and Community Development Act of 1977	95th (HR 6655, PL 128)	0.5505	0.2276
Department of Housing and Urban Development Reform Act of 1989	101st (HR 1, PL 235)	0.2506	0.2967
Emergency Housing Act of 1975	94th (HR 5398, PL 50)	0.149	0.3393
National Housing Act Amendment of 1982	97th (HR 6038, PL 185)	1.399	0.5791
Joint resolution: National Housing Act Amendments of 1974	93rd (SJR 263, PL 93-541)	2.068	0.6967

emergency relief for mortgage indebtedness; the corporation was established by Congress for three years. Of more lasting importance, the act established federal savings and loan associations (SLAs), which sought to encourage saving and home financing, and converted members of the Federal Home Loan Bank into federally chartered SLAs, thereby expanding the regulatory power of the federal government.

A significant but not nearly as important bill was the Housing Act of 1954. This bill, championed by President Eisenhower, sought to encourage the elimination of slums by providing insurance for the rehabilitation of existing dwellings and encouraging the construction of public housing to replace dwellings demolished in the process of urban renewal. The most important effect of the bill was its emphasis on urban development and its concomitant retreat from the provision of public housing. It rates relatively high on the significance scale, yet is not as influential a piece of legislation as the other enactments discussed here.

Of less importance were the Housing and Community Development Act of 1977 and the Department of Housing and Urban Development (HUD) Reform Act of 1989. The former bill included substantial changes to the community development block grant, provided for a number of studies on urban development, and extended provisions established in prior bills. The primary aim of the latter bill, which amended a variety of laws concerning housing and community development, was to reform the accountability and management of the Department of Housing and Urban Development and the Federal Housing Administration. The impetus for this bill was concern over the management of HUD under Secretary Samuel R. Pierce Jr.: officials in the department, through numerous programs that allowed for the allocation of funds based on personal discretion, were providing housing subsidies to developers on the basis of political favoritism.

The last three bills are of considerably less importance. The Emergency Housing Act of 1975 provided temporary assistance in the form of emergency loans and advances in order to limit the extent of the foreclosures occurring at that time as a result of recession and high interest rates. It was a significantly watered-down bill relative to an earlier version vetoed by President Gerald Ford, and the activities of the authority established under the act were limited to one year. It nevertheless scores higher than the National Housing Act Amendment of 1982, a one-sentence bill that changed section 235(h)(1) of the National Housing Act to read "September 30, 1982" in lieu of "March 31, 1982," or the joint resolution (PL 93-541) that clarified the authority of the Federal Savings and Loan Insurance Corporation and the National Housing Act. Neither of these public laws were of any significance, and this is reflected in their respective scores.

Table 5.4 provides a list of ten enactments relating to agriculture policy. Overall, the same face validity of the significance ranking is observed when we examine bills in this policy area. Once again, many of the more significant bills were passed during the New Deal. The Agricultural Adjustment Act of 1933 was a very important piece of legislation that created the Agricultural Adjustment Administration and restricted agricultural production by provid- ing subsidies to farmers for growing fewer crops and raising fewer animals. The objective of establishing parity between the production and consumption of agricultural products and increasing the purchasing power of farmers was accomplished by levying a tax on the domestic processing of particular crops. This policy led to the Agricultural Adjustment Administration being declared unconstitutional by the Supreme Court in 1936.[14]

The 1933 act, however, went far beyond establishing the Agricultural Adjustment Administration and increasing the purchasing power of pro- ducers. It also provided for a massive refinancing of agricultural debt and farm mortgages, provided $100 million in loans for joint-stock land banks and $200 million in direct loans to farmers, increased the lending power of the Reconstruction Finance Corporation (RFC), and greatly expanded the

---

[14] *United States v. Butler*, 297 U.S. 1 (1936).

Table 5.4 Examples of Agricultural Enactments

Title	Congress	Estimate	Standard Error
Agricultural Adjustment Act of 1933	73rd (HR 3835, PL 10)	1.707	0.3359
Agricultural Marketing Act of 1929	71st (HR 1, PL 10)	1.499	0.3053
Grazing Act of 1934	73rd (HR 6465, PL 482)	1.405	0.2981
Federal Farm Loan Act of 1916	64th (S 2986, PL 158)	1.398	0.3018
Farm Credit Act of 1933	73rd (HR 5790, PL 75)	1.216	0.2759
Soil Conservation and Domestic Allotment Act of 1936	74th (S 3780, PL 461)	1.168	0.274
Bureau of Animal Industry Act of 1884	48th (HR 3967)	0.9286	0.259
1921 joint resolution compensating Cotton Belt states for pink bollworm eradication	67th (SJR 72, Resolution 12)	−1.175	0.6062
1940 amendment to Sugar Act of 1937	76th (S 3237, PL 660)	−1.582	0.6806
Joint resolution: Angora goat report of 1905	58th (HJR 193, Resolution 24)	−2.09	0.7255

authority of the president to regulate the value of U.S. currency. As noted by the *New York Times*, this bill alone empowered the president with "the widest range of authority over the economic affairs of the nation ever granted to a President in peace time," in one measure granting "unprecedented control over agricultural production and marketing, refinancing for billions of dollars of agricultural debts and a complete adjustment of the currency system of the United States".[15] This was a landmark piece of legislation whose broad significance and lasting impact have solidified its position at the top of the list of agricultural legislation.

Another important bill, this one passed before the New Deal, was the 1929 Agricultural Marketing Act, which established the Federal Farm Board. The objectives of this bill, drafted in response to the growing agricultural crisis, were to minimize speculation, encourage the organization of farmers into corporations, prevent inefficient methods of distribution, and prevent the production of crop surpluses and their depreciating effect on prices. The bill— hailed by President Herbert Hoover as "the most important measure passed in

[15]"President Signs Farm Bill, Making Inflation the Law," *New York Times*, May 13, 1933.

aid of a single industry"—significantly restructured the agricultural industry in the United States by encouraging the formation of farmers' cooperatives.[16]

The 1934 Grazing Act provided the secretary of the Interior with broad powers to protect and preserve public ranges and was the first act to regulate grazing on public land. It created grazing districts within the public range where local ranchers could obtain a lease for their stock to graze. The bill established the Division of Grazing in the Department of Interior to carry out the provisions of the act. Later renamed the U.S. Grazing Service, this division merged in 1946 with the General Land Office to become the Bureau of Land Management (BLM). An act of similar importance was the 1916 Federal Farm Loan Act, which sought to provide capital for agricultural development and to equalize rates of interest on farm loans. The bill created twelve federal land bank districts for members of national farm loan associations (NFLAs), with each land and joint-stock bank organized under this act being a depository of public money. Farmers could borrow from these banks using their land as collateral, thereby increasing the availability of capital for agriculture. Furthermore, the bill established the Federal Farm Loan Bureau and the Federal Farm Loan Board to administer the provisions of the bill.

Of somewhat less importance were the Farm Credit Act of 1933 and the 1936 Soil Conservation and Domestic Allotment Act. The former created one central and numerous local "banks for cooperatives" that could loan money to cooperatives subject to the provisions and limitations of the Agricultural Marketing Act, which itself was amended by this bill. The Agricultural Marketing Act authorized the secretary of Agriculture to conduct surveys and take conservation measures, such as providing financial assistance to farmers, and it sought to raise the purchasing power of farmers while promoting conservation and the improvement of soil fertility. States that submitted plans for the achievement of these objectives were eligible for grants from the federal government. Some sections of the act were to be administered by the Agricultural Adjustment Administration, which was amended by this bill to respond to the Supreme Court's judgment that its activities were unconstitutional.

The 1884 Bureau of Animal Industry Act, drafted in response to the spread of pleuro-pneumonia, established the bureau within the Department of Agriculture. The bureau was given the authority to inspect all livestock in the United States, and exporting or transporting diseased animals became misdemeanors punishable by fines of $100 to $5,000 or imprisonment not to exceed one year. The bill was of limited importance, and its most important feature was the establishment of the Bureau of Animal Industry.

The last three bills were of very little importance and are accordingly placed near the bottom of the significance ranking. The 1921 joint resolution called for aid to the southern states that had given relief to farmers forced from their

---

[16] "Hoover Signs the Farm Relief Bill," *New York Times*, June 16, 1929.

Table 5.5 Top 100 Enactments

Title	Congress	Estimate	Standard Error
Federal Trade Commission Act of 1914	63rd (HR 15613, PL 203)	2.310	0.4777
Tariff of 1909	61st (HR 1438, PL 5)	2.120	0.4271
Pure Food and Drug Act of 1906	59th (S 88, PL 384)	1.956	0.3645
Federal Reserve Act of 1913	63rd (HR 7837, PL 43)	1.946	0.3694
Social Security Act of 1935	74th (HR 7260, PL 271)	1.912	0.3953
Anti-Trust Act of 1890	51st (S 1)	1.901	0.3621
Tariff Act of 1930	71st (HR 2667, PL 361)	1.888	0.3658
Labor Management Relations Act of 1947	80th (HR 3020, PL 101)	1.887	0.3964
Securities Exchange Act of 1934	73rd (HR 9323, PL 291)	1.833	0.3566
Commerce Court established in 1910	61st (HR 17536, PL 218)	1.831	0.3604
National Industrial Recovery Act of 1933	73rd (HR 5755, PL 67)	1.754	0.3363
Tariff of 1894	53rd (HR 4864)	1.750	0.3465
Inter-State Commerce Act of 1887	49th (S1532)	1.744	0.3333
Interstate commerce regulations of 1906	59th (HR 12987, PL 337)	1.743	0.3279
An Act to Promote the Defense of the United States of 1941	77th (HR 1776, PL 11)	1.739	0.3370
Agricultural Adjustment Act of 1933	73rd (HR 3835, PL 10)	1.707	0.3359
Tariff of 1897	55th (HR 379)	1.698	0.3289
Amendment to the Internal Revenue Code of 1954	97th (HR 4242, PL 34)	1.695	0.4239
National Labor Relations Act of 1935	74th (S 1958, PL 198)	1.695	0.3597
U.S. Housing Act of 1937	75th (S 1685, PL 412)	1.684	0.3346
Tennessee Valley Authority Act of 1933	73rd (HR 5081, PL 17)	1.682	0.3109
Anti-Trust Act of 1914	63rd (HR 15657, PL 212)	1.679	0.3276
Civil Service Act of 1883	47th (S 133)	1.676	0.3214
Tariff of 1913	63rd (HR 3321, PL 16)	1.673	0.3217
Agricultural Adjustment Act of 1938	75th (HR 8505, PL 430)	1.671	0.3385
Employment Act of 1946	79th (S 380, PL 304)	1.656	0.3580

Table 5.5 Continued.

Title	Congress	Estimate	Standard Error
Army emergency increase of 1917	65th (HR 3545, PL 12)	1.654	0.3308
Fair Labor Standards Act of 1938	75th (S 2475, PL 718)	1.650	0.3212
Silver dollar established in 1878	45th (HR 1093)	1.634	0.3478
Immigration Act of 1924	68th (HR 7995, PL 139)	1.601	0.3013
Banking Act of 1935	74th (HR 7617, PL 305)	1.599	0.3214
Chinese Immigration of 1882	47th (HR 5804)	1.578	0.3235
Child Labor Act of 1916	64th (HR 8234, PL 249)	1.573	0.3183
Securities Act of 1933	73rd (HR 5480, PL 22)	1.565	0.3087
National Prohibition Act of 1919	66th (HR 6810, PL 66)	1.564	0.3036
Public Utility Act of 1935	74th (S 2796, PL 333)	1.557	0.2864
Trade Agreements Act of 1934	73rd (HR 8687, PL 316)	1.551	0.2986
Transportation Act of 1920	66th (HR 10453, PL 152)	1.537	0.3191
National Housing Act of 1934	73th (HR 9620, PL 479)	1.524	0.3289
Irrigation Act of 1902	57th (S 3057)	1.524	0.3110
Civil Rights Act of 1964	88th (HR 7152, PL 352)	1.508	0.3172
Amendment to the Internal Revenue Code of 1954 to reduce individual and corporate income taxes and make structural changes in the income tax	88th (HR 8363, PL 272)	1.505	0.3352
Agricultural Marketing Act of 1929	71st (HR 1, PL 10)	1.499	0.3053
National Commission on Social Security Reform of 1983	98th (HR 1900, PL 21)	1.475	0.3404
Reconstruction Finance Corporation Act of 1932	72nd (HR 7360, PL 2)	1.472	0.3073
Federal Aid Road Act of 1956	84th (HR 10660, PL 627)	1.464	0.3335
Finance Act of 1900	56th (HR 1)	1.452	0.2826
Gramm-Rudman-Hollings Act of 1985	99th (HJR 372, PL 177)	1.450	0.3264
Revenue Act of 1942	77th (HR 7378, PL 753)	1.449	0.3090
Tariff of 1890	51st (HR 9416)	1.448	0.3013
Emergency Quota Act of 1921 Limited of 1921	67th (HR 4075, PL 5)	1.424	0.2834
Housing Act of 1961	87th (S1922, PL 70),	1.418	0.2856

Table 5.5 Continued.

Title	Congress	Estimate	Standard Error
Social Security Amendments of 1965 (Medicare)	89th (HR 6675, PL 97)	1.409	0.2861
Federal Emergency Relief Act of 1933	73rd (HR 4606, PL 15)	1.406	0.2912
Grazing Act of 1934	73rd (HR 6462, PL 482)	1.405	0.2981
Silver Act of 1890	51st (HR 5381)	1.399	0.2891
War Labor Disputes Act of 1943	78th (S 796, PL 89)	1.399	0.2896
Federal Farm Loan Act of 1916	64th (S 2986, PL 158)	1.398	0.3018
Emergency banking relief provided in Emergency Banking Act of 1933	73rd (HR 1491, PL 1)	1.382	0.2861
Gold Reserve Act of 1934	73rd (HR 6976, PL 87)	1.372	0.2810
Reduction of Internal Revenue taxes in 1883	47th (HR 5538)	1.369	0.2886
Provision in 1965 for the nation's elementary and secondary schools to strengthen and improve educational quality and educational opportunities	89th (HR 2362, PL 10)	1.349	0.2855
Tax Reform Act of 1969	91st (HR 13270, PL 172)	1.326	0.2664
Prohibition Act of 1917	65th (SJR 17, constitutional amendment)	1.306	0.2867
Atomic Energy Act of 1946	79th (S 1717, PL 585)	1.305	0.2841
Tariff Act of 1922	67th (HR 7456, PL 318)	1.298	0.2645
National Bank Circulation Act of 1908	60th (HR 21871, PL 169)	1.297	0.2811
Banking Act of 1933	73rd (HR 5661, PL 66)	1.295	0.2810
Federal Home Loan Bank Act of 1932	72nd (HR 12280, PL 304)	1.293	0.2692
Interstate Commerce and Liability of Corporations Act of 1903	57th (S 7053)	1.292	0.2781
Home Owners' Loan Act of 1933	73rd (HR 5240, PL 43)	1.290	0.2730
Selective Training and Service Act of 1940	76th (S 4164, PL 783)	1.290	0.2730
Enforce the 15th Amendment to the Constitution Relating to the Right to Vote, 1965	89th (S 1564, PL 110)	1.281	0.2550

Table 5.5 Continued.

Title	Congress	Estimate	Standard Error
Packers and Stockyards Act of 1921	67th (HR 6320, PL 51)	1.274	0.2644
Philippine Government Act of 1902	57th (S 2295)	1.272	0.2629
Federal Reserve System and Facilities Act of 1932	72nd (HR 9203, PL 44)	1.272	0.2852
Mobilize the Human and Financial Resources of the Nation to Combat Poverty in the United States, 1964	88th (S 2642, PL 452)	1.266	0.2788
Reorganization Act of 1939	76th (HR 4425, PL 19)	1.262	0.2568
National Defense Act of 1916	64th (HR 12766, PL 85)	1.257	0.2748
Eight-Hour Workday Act of 1916	64th (HR 17700, PL 252)	1.257	0.2727
Independence of Cuba Act of 1898	55th (HR 233)	1.256	0.2711
Hatch Act of 1939	76th (S 1871, PL 252)	1.254	0.2809
Income Tax Act of 1909	61st (SJR 40, constitutional amendment)	1.251	0.2719
Rural Electrification Act of 1936	74th (S 3483, PL 605)	1.251	0.2814
Prevent Certain Abuses in Labor Organizations Act of 1959	86th (S 1555, PL 257)	1.248	0.2784
World War Adjusted Compensation Act of 1924	68th (HR 7959, PL 120)	1.241	0.2617
Communications Satellite Act of 1962	87th (HR 11040, PL 624)	1.239	0.2599
Silver Purchase Act of 1934	73rd (HR 9745, PL 438)	1.238	0.2649
Provision in 1972 of fiscal assistance to states and local governments	92nd (HR 14370, PL 512)	1.232	0.2635
Foreign Assistance Act of 1948	80th (S 2202, PL 472)	1.231	0.2810
Repeal of Silver Purchases Act of 1893	53rd (HR 1)	1.216	0.2663
Farm Credit Act of 1933	73rd (HR 5790, PL 75)	1.216	0.2759
Copyrights Act of 1891	51st (HR 10881)	1.206	0.2663
Miscellaneous changes in the tax laws, 1982	97th (HR 4961, PL 248)	1.202	0.2897
Espionage Act of 1917	65th (HR 291, PL 24)	1.201	0.2695

Table 5.5 Continued.

Title	Congress	Estimate	Standard Error
Department of Commerce and Labor Act of 1903	57th (S 569)	1.197	0.2665
Amendment to the Atomic Energy Act of 1954	83rd (HR 9757, PL 703)	1.192	0.2978
Revenue Act of 1916	64th (HR 16763, PL 271)	1.186	0.2696
Espionage Offenses Act of 1918	65th (HR 8753, PL 150)	1.184	0.2839
Disability and Pensions Act of 1890	51st (S 389)	1.177	0.2545

fields by efforts to eliminate the pink bollworm. The 1940 amendment to the Sugar Act authorized the secretary to deduct $10 from payments to producers for each day in which a child was employed contrary to the provisions of the act. The 1905 joint resolution provided for the publication of three thousand copies of bulletin 27 of the Bureau of Animal Industry, entitled "Information Concerning the Angora Goat."

Though space does not permit a full discussion, very reasonable significance rankings are observed across the entire set of issue areas. The top one hundred significant laws are listed in table 5.5. This table allows the reader to check the face validity of the significance estimates.

CONSTRUCTING MACRO-LEVEL MEASURES OF LEGISLATIVE ACCOMPLISHMENT

How can individual statute–level significance estimates be used to construct a measure of legislative accomplishment, and how can the policy substance issue coding described in chapter 2 be leveraged to construct additional policy-specific measures of legislative accomplishment that would be valuable?

There are essentially two approaches to the construction of measures of legislative accomplishment from the significance data. The first is to *sum significance scores* for all legislation or subsets of legislation. For example, the significance scores of the 37,766 laws passed by Congress from 1877 to 1994 can be summed to produce a Congress-by-Congress measure of overall legislative accomplishment. Such a measure can also be broken down by policy issue area. For example, between 1877 and 1994, Congress enacted 5,491 statutes having to do with what have been classified as international affairs issues. These statutes could be summed, Congress by Congress, to construct an overall measure of legislative accomplishment for international affairs. The alternative approach to summing individual significance scores is to produce a *count measure* of legislative accomplishment—that is, a simple count of laws passed by Congress. This measure can also be broken down by either policy issue area or any other threshold of significance. In practice, summing and counting are empirically indistinguishable measures because they correlate at (or above) the 0.99 level. I use the count measure in this book because it is easier to interpret.[17]

To illustrate exactly how the legislative accomplishment measures are constructed, consider a specific example: a measure based on the top 500 statutes enacted by Congress. This top-500 measure consists of the 500 public laws enacted between 1877 and 1994 with the highest significance scores.[18] Each Congress is a count of how many of the top 500 laws were enacted during that Congress. The range of this measure varies from 0 to 29 enactments. The highlights of the top 500 significant enactments include the 73rd Congress (1933–34), President Roosevelt's first, which ushered in the New Deal with a series high of 29 major enactments, and President Johnson's 89th Congress (1965–66), which passed 19 major enactments. Four Congresses have the negative distinction of passing no enactments from the top-500 list: the 46th (1879–81), the 54th (1895–97), the 58th (1903–5) and the 100th (1987–88).

It is also possible to construct measures broken down by policy substance. For example, 319 (of the top 500) enactments are classified as domestic affairs and 89 as international affairs. Figure 5.1 provide a graphic representation of the top 500 statutes overall and broken down by policy issue area (international affairs and domestic affairs).

Of course, we are not limited to relying upon the top 500 statutes. Determining the correct threshold is largely dependent on the questions at hand. It might be appropriate to use a more inclusive threshold, such as the top 3,500, to study the growth of the state/administrative capacity in the twentieth century.[19] Figure 5.2 provides a breakdown of legislative accomplishment for the top 3,500 statutes and for the four tier 1 policy issue categories: sovereignty, organization and scope, international affairs, and domestic affairs.

---

[17] Although the summation of significance scores measure is, in principle, superior (see Clinton and Lapinski 2006), the ease of interpreting count measures makes them preferable because they are simply summations of enactments. A count measure is easier to interpret because it is easy to understand multivariate findings that translate into x more enactments instead of x more significance score points. And of course, because analyses are conducted on subsets of highly significant laws, the count measure still incorporates the information from the significance scores. The individual-level significance scores are leveraged here because subset lists of important enactments across different thresholds (for example, the top 500 enactments, the top 1,000, or the top 3,500) could not be constructed without the individual-level scores.

[18] A measure of the top 500 enactments is nearly equivalent to the list of landmark enactments produced by David Mayhew in *Divided We Govern* (1991), except that this measure covers an additional thirty-five Congresses (over seventy years).

[19] The top-3,500 threshold is particularly appealing because 3,591 statutes of the total 37,766 were rated as important by at least one rater.

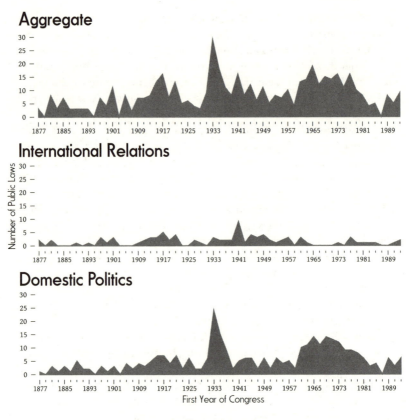

Figure 5.1
Top 500 Enactments, 1877 to 1993

What is clearly evident from the figures is that the measures of accomplishment vary across issues (and thresholds). Here it should be noted that if the correlations between sovereignty, organization and scope, international affairs, and domestic affairs are assessed for the top 3,500 enactments, correlations that range from 0.13 to 0.67 are observed. Here, sovereignty is correlated at 0.13 with organization and scope, at 0.05 with international affairs, and at 0.00 with domestic affairs. The highest correlation of 0.67 is between international and domestic affairs. Organization and scope is correlated with international and domestic affairs at the 0.40 and 0.45 levels, respectively. The correlations of the measures become even weaker when shifted to a threshold of the top 500. The notable change observed when shifting thresholds from the top 3,500 to the top 500 enactments is between international and domestic affairs. This correlation drops to 0.12, and no other individual policy-specific correlation is higher than 0.23.

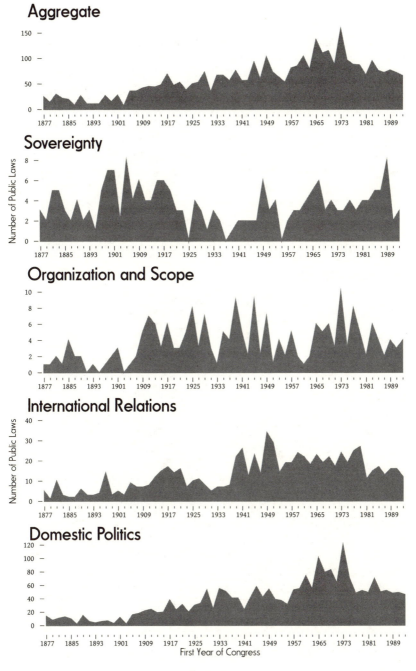

Figure 5.2
Top 3,500 Enactments, 1877 to 1993

CONCLUSION

This chapter has presented a novel and critical new measure of lawmaking that can serve as a key indicator for how lawmaking behaves across different historical periods in the United States. It is particularly important to have direct measures of lawmaking given that almost everything we know empirically about lawmaking is derived from roll call–based measures, which are imperfect proxy variables for studying lawmaking. The next chapter determines the specific costs of excluding policy issue substance from our study of lawmaking by turning to a multivariate analysis of the legislative accomplishment data broken down by policy issue area.

Chapter VI

Explaining Lawmaking in the United States, 1877–1994

IN THIS CHAPTER, I examine variations in lawmaking by specific issue areas at the macro level.[1] Drawing on both the general and issue-specific measures of legislative accomplishment developed in chapter 5, this chapter empirically demonstrates that theoretically important determinants of lawmaking do not work the same way across policy issue areas. The findings highlight how easy it is to mischaracterize the policymaking process by not disaggregating policy into theoretically relevant categories. I also show in this chapter the importance of incorporating issue substance for constructing preference-based determinants of lawmaking. In other words, not taking policy issue substance into account in our analyses of lawmaking often leads us to get it partially right or wrong in multiple ways.

This chapter's assessment of the determinants of lawmaking relies heavily on the Congress literature, since the American political development and policy studies literatures offer few empirically testable explanatory accounts of lawmaking. The Congress subfield provides the determinants and hypotheses in this chapter, but it is usually silent on how lawmaking might vary by policy issue area. The empirical findings presented here demonstrate that policy substance is nonetheless very important for lawmaking and suggest that insights from the APD subfield in particular are useful in better understanding the causal mechanisms in different policy issue areas. APD suggests clear ways to parse policy by policy issue area according to theoretical principles, and key determinants of lawmaking appear to vary systematically across issue domains that are largely informed by APD ideas. Consequently, while APD might not yet offer a well-defined theoretical framework to explain lawmaking across these issue areas, it does provide us with the ideas necessary to build a framework that can be used to interpret differences in empirical regularities in lawmaking across well-justified policy categories. This is a critical first step to building rigorous theories about lawmaking across issue areas.

---

[1] This chapter is adapted from and extends Lapinski (2008).

After introducing the hypotheses tested in this chapter and explaining the covariates used to assess them, I briefly reintroduce the measures of legislative accomplishment constructed in chapter 5—which serve as the dependent variables used in the multivariate analyses—and explain why studying actual legislative output instead of the entire policy issue agenda is justifiable to study the lawmaking process. I then present and interpret the findings of the multivariate empirical analyses and discuss the empirical findings.

CRITICAL HYPOTHESES AND COVARIATES OF LAWMAKING

Can government legislate significant policy change, and if so, under what conditions? This vital question has interested political scientists ever since it was first asked. It is also a question that is revisited by pundits and the media every year. In this section, I evaluate these two questions and introduce a number of testable hypotheses that students of Congress and lawmaking consider important. These hypotheses are implicitly interesting to APD scholars given that lawmaking provides the backbone to the American state. These hypotheses are directly related to important formal and informal accounts of lawmaking. Although an important goal of this chapter, is empirically assessing theoretical propositions, it is equally important to determine empirical generalizations for lawmaking across theoretically coherent policy issue areas.

Understanding empirical regularities in this type of work is important because such knowledge helps us build better micro-foundations for modeling the lawmaking process. Consequently, the work here is somewhat akin to early work within the economics subfield of industrial organization (IO), which, though now highly regarded, was once considered a weak area (Mason and Lamont 1982; Tirole 1988). During a long growing period, careful inductive work in the IO subfield was conducted through many industry-specific qualitative case studies, followed by rigorous empirical analyses. After gaining a firm understanding of how individual firms behave, the work became more theoretical and focused on efficiency and profits. Political scientists, likewise, are just beginning to fully appreciate how lawmaking works, especially by policy issue area. Thus, while some of the work presented in this chapter is somewhat exploratory in nature, I would argue that it is nonetheless very useful for assessing as well as building explanatory accounts of the lawmaking process.

It is important to recognize that even with the immense data collection and measurement issues addressed in this book, only fifty-nine (Congresses) observations are in the data set. Although these Congresses cover a time span of 118 years, nevertheless, it would not be prudent to attempt to include every possible explanation and related covariate in the model specifications; doing so would lead quickly to saturation and no degrees of freedom. Instead, I adopt a parsimonious specification that includes the most common and important covariates found in the literature. In other words, I include important and theoretically implied covariates in the specification for the multivariate analyses and leave out other covariates that are neither amenable to measurement nor theoretically relevant. The covariates included in the analysis differ, however, from other studies of lawmaking. The largest difference comes in the polarization measure, which is constructed by policy issue area. The idea here is that better measures of polarization will allow for a more accurate (and less attenuated) portrayal of how polarization affects lawmaking.

Additionally, it is not the purpose of this chapter to serve as a horse race for the favorite covariates of Congress scholars. Rather than blindly assess differently specified models against each other to see which performs better, I use what I believe is a well-specified but sparse model to test a number of prominent formal and informal accounts of lawmaking. Included in the analysis are theoretically appropriate variables in the supply and demand of public policies, which are likely to vary by both policy issue substance and significance threshold across a number of different measures of legislative accomplishment. There should be no surprises here: the covariates I discuss are well known among Congress scholars.

Theoretically Implied Covariates

In explaining covariates that address the causal mechanisms associated with lawmaking and are amenable to measurement and analysis, I comment, where appropriate, on when we might not expect a covariate to behave the same across different policy issue areas. It is important to remind the reader that some explanatory accounts of lawmaking that are not measurable across the entire time period analyzed (1877 to 1994), such as public mood (Erikson, MacKuen and Stimson 2002; Mayhew 1991), are beyond the analytic scope of this chapter.

Gridlock Covariates

Students of Congress and lawmaking, as well as the news media, have given an immense amount of attention to elite polarization, which is thought to be a primary causal source of policy gridlock in Washington. Consequently, polarization is included in the specification. For comparison purposes, two types of polarization are used. The first, an aggregate measure of polarization, measures the distance between the Democratic Party and Republican Party median of the roll call–based DW-NOMINATE scores (McCarty, Poole, and Rosenthal 2006).[2] I also construct this measure using the aggregate mean

---

[2] I use first-dimension NOMINATE scores.

preference standardized scores introduced in chapter 4. The standardized ideal points generated through the procedure outlined by Groseclose et al. (1999) and outlined in chapter 3 produce two versions of the standardized scores. The mean preference score used in this chapter is more highly correlated with NOMINATE.[3] In addition, I use the issue-specific measures of polarization also introduced in chapter 4. The issue-based scores of polarization are the mean preference standardized scores broken down by tier 1 issue category.[4] The idea is to correctly measure polarization by policy area—the same idea advocated by Krehbiel and his colleagues (2005)—in order to avoid the consequences of measurement error. The measures of polarization used here are often viewed as a proxy for the gridlock interval proposed by the pivotal politics model of Krehbiel (1998) and Brady and Volden (1998). Consequently, scholars often think that inclusion of a polarization covariate is an implicit test of the pivotal politics theory of lawmaking. This polarization hypothesis, labeled H1, is that polarization decreases legislative accomplishment.

H1: The higher the level of elite polarization, the less legislative accomplishment.

Although it is often hypothesized that polarization in Congress reduces legislative productivity, it is not clear whether elite polarization has an impact on legislative productivity across all types of policy. For example, is the causal mechanism for elite polarization the same for issues that are considered "off cleavage" and therefore are not structured by the traditional ideological splits of the dominant two-party system?[5] Important historical work suggests that intraparty splits are critical for lawmaking. For example, sovereignty issues— which, according to our coding schema, include laws related to civil rights, boundaries, membership, and liberty—have often involved intraparty and regional splits; in the same vein, the split between southern and northern Democrats, not interparty conflict, is considered by some to have had a more important effect on civil rights legislation (Katznelson, Geiger, and Kryder 1993).

In addition to polarization, I include a covariate to capture divided control of government. As mentioned earlier, David Mayhew's (1991) work on the consequences of divided government was absolutely pioneering, not for its theoretical offerings, but for providing a first cut at the complicated task of

---

[3] Given that an important point of this chapter is to explore differences between using aggregated and disaggregated measures, I decided to use the mean preference scores, since they are empirically more similar to NOMINATE. The aggregate analyses are highly sensitive to this choice. Future collaborative research will explore differences between NOMINATE and Bayesian-based measures.

[4] The primary point of this move is to empirically demonstrate that a Bayesian aggregate measure of ideal points is similar to a DW-NOMINATE-based measure.

[5] Some accounts suggest that polarization leads to personal animosity that might hamper the ability of legislators to work together. If this is the case, we might not expect polarization to behave differently across policy issues.

measuring governmental performance—here measured as the productivity of important legislation—over a long time horizon. His simple count of public laws, which makes the critical distinction between landmark legislation and everything else, challenges the long-standing belief that unified party government leads to moments of high legislative productivity while divided government contributes to legislative gridlock.

Mayhew's controversial work on the determinants of lawmaking opened up an extensive and interesting debate on the effect of unified and divided government, making the study of divided government without question the most active area of research in the study of lawmaking during the 1990s. The idea, posited by others (Cutler 1988; Sundquist 1988) and first rigorously empirically tested by Mayhew (1991), is that split control of government reduces the likelihood of enacting legislation.

> H2: Legislative accomplishment should be lower during periods of divided govern-
> ment than in periods of unified government.

Divided government is an indicator for whether the same party controls both chambers of Congress as well as the presidency.[6] Like the work on polarization, robust theoretical work that provides a framework for understanding how divided government might affect lawmaking differently by policy issue area has not been undertaken.

Demand-Related Covariates (Opportunities for Change)

In an attempt to capture the impact of exogenous shocks to the legislative environment, I include war in the specification. Operationalized as an indicator variable, this variable includes only "hot" wars (Mayhew 2005b): the Spanish-American War, World War I, World War II, the Korean War, the Vietnam War, and the Gulf War. The Vietnam War is separated out from the rest of the series because of a number of coincident changes in the environment over the period. Consequently, there are two war-related variables—one indicator variable that includes all wars except Vietnam and a separate indicator variable for Vietnam.

War is expected to significantly increase the productivity of international affairs legislation, but the expectation of this variable for domestic politics is somewhat unclear. Domestic affairs legislation related to war efforts might be expected to increase, but a crowding-out effect might lead to either no change or a decrease in other types of laws. There is very little theoretical or empirical work on the subject, so, although it is reasonable to suppose that war affects

---

[6]In related work, John Coleman (1999) hypothesizes that unified Democratic government is more likely to lead to an increase in legislative productivity than unified Republican government. This idea is not empirically explored in this book.

policy production, we have no good understanding of how it should do so.[7] Consequently, I do not state a formal hypothesis for this section.

Theoretically Important Control Variables

Majority party advantage is the difference in size between the majority and minority parties in the House. This variable measures the resources that a party may have at its disposal and might be interpreted as a proxy for public sentiment in that it captures how strongly the country is behind the majority party.

Start of term is an indicator variable for the first Congress of each presidential term. The variable takes a value of 1 for every other Congress. Mayhew (1991, 177) includes start of term as a control with "the idea that more laws are likely to pass during the first half of a four-year presidential term than during the second half." Krehbiel (1998) elaborates on this idea by noting the relation between legislative productivity and the width of the gridlock interval. In other words, this covariate might be capturing changes in the number of movable status quos available to Congress.

Time is included to account for systematic changes in the environment that are not captured by the included covariates. Including this variable accounts for any trends in the country over the period. For example, a trend would control for the rise of the administrative state and/or the possibility that as Congress passes additional landmark laws it creates the opportunity for seriously amending them later on. Interpreting precisely what the trend captures is clearly impossible, but time is nonetheless an important control because it captures the changing institutional and societal environments in which Congress operates across the time period.[8]

EMPIRICALLY ANALYZING LAWMAKING

The empirical core of this chapter—the multivariate analysis—aims to determine whether pooling policies is inappropriate when studying lawmaking. In analyzing the determinants of lawmaking, do we mask or dampen important

---

[7]It might also be argued—as Stephen Skowronek does in his book *The Politics Presidents Make* (1997)—that the longer a regime is in power, the less can be done legislatively. The idea is that a regime would change as many of the status quo policies as possible (given the preferences of Congress and the president), leaving no remaining policies to be changed. Others have argued that given the number of legislative reauthorizations and expirations, this is not a problem. Given the other controls in the analysis, time in power is omitted from the analyses presented in the multivariate section. As a robustness check, all the models were run with a time-in-power variable, and in no case did the inclusion of this variable substantively change the results.

[8]$Time^2$ is too highly correlated with polarization to be included.

relationships when we pool policy types instead of disaggregating them? The answer to this question has important implications for testing current accounts of lawmaking.

The dependent variable in the analyses, a sum of the number of laws passed Congress by Congress, is broken down by legislative significance and policy issue area. The measure is explained in detail in chapter 5. For example, between 1877 and 1994 Congress enacted 5,491 statutes that have been classified as international affairs issues. These statutes could be summed Congress by Congress to construct an overall measure of legislative accomplishment for international affairs. This chapter uses two thresholds of significance for analysis, including measures of legislative accomplishment based on the top 3,500 and the top 500 enactments. Although choosing a threshold for analysis is somewhat arbitrary, choosing these two is justified since the top 3,500 leverages heavily the 3,591 public laws that were deemed important by at least one expert rater and essentially captures all legislation of extremely high to moderate importance and the top 500 parallels the threshold used by Mayhew (1991) in *Divided We Govern.*

One more issue needs to be addressed before moving to the multivariate analyses, namely, whether it is appropriate to study the legislative process by focusing exclusively on the amount of legislation enacted by a given Congress instead of on how much of its political agenda a Congress enacted.

The "Denominator" Problem: Statutes Versus the Agenda

A controversy within the literature of lawmaking is often referred to as the "denominator" problem. David Mayhew (2006) has commented extensively on this topic, so the discussion here is limited to only essential points. The controversy concerns whether one should focus on the numerator as well as the denominator in assessing legislative performance (Binder 2003). Those who believe it is necessary to focus on both are referred to here as "ratio" advocates. These scholars argue that the differing sizes of political agendas (the denominator) must be accounted for if legislative accomplishment is to be truly measured because the size of the agenda is related to the opportunities to legislate. Thus, if the agenda is small, it is not possible to pass a large number of consequential legislations. If a Congress with a large agenda passes only a few major enactments, ratio advocates would consider such a Congress unproductive. On the other hand, if Congress passes only a few major enactments but the agenda is limited (for instance, Woodrow Wilson's initial 63rd Congress, 1913–15), then this Congress would be considered highly accomplished because the laws passed in relation to the size of the agenda produce a very high ratio (passed laws to agenda size). It is not the point of this study to determine whether a ratio-dependent variable is valuable under some circumstances; others have better addressed this issue (see Binder 2003;

Mayhew 2006). Instead, I argue here simply that using only the numerator is a very good measure of legislative accomplishment and is not problematic, primarily because, the assumption that the opportunities for legislating are identical across time is made only after making it conditional on including control covariates in the analysis. This is a critical point that others, especially Binder (1999, 2003), fail to address. Including these covariates implicitly precludes the assumption that the opportunities for changing the status quo are constant. Indeed, these covariates are included precisely to control for differences in the size of the agenda a Congress faces.

A key idea introduced in this book is that opportunities to legislate vary by policy substance, since such opportunities are linked to how events, among other factors, are likely to alter the distribution of movable status quos in different issue areas. In other words, opportunities to legislate vary according to political context and by policy substance. Including appropriate covariates in the model can account for the possibility that the size of the lawmaking agenda changes and/or that a Congress has more or fewer opportunities to alter policy. For example, involvement in a war changes the political environment and brings issues onto the political agenda that would not otherwise have appeared there. By altering the distribution of movable status quo points, wars may also change the opportunities for passing certain policies. Of course, other controls (covariates) may also be necessary. For example, some have argued that there are more opportunities for passing legislation in the first two years of a presidential term than in the final two, which means that including such a control accounts for differences in the number of movable status quos (Mayhew 1991).

Multivariate Analyses

Because the dependent variables analyzed are counts of significant enactments in particular Congresses, the relationship is modeled using a negative binomial regression model.[9]

As explained earlier, seven covariates are included in the models: these measures capture polarization, divided government, the majority party advantage, start-of-term effects, war, and secular trends via a time trend. Table 6.1 provides the results using my aggregate measure of political polarization for the top 500 and top 3,500 laws as well as a DW-NOMINATE measure of polarization.

The results show that the findings between the models are similar, though there are differences across legislative productivity thresholds. One clear

---

[9]When appropriate, a simple poisson process is substituted for the negative binomial model, which otherwise is appropriate for count data. The poisson is substituted for the negative binomial when there is no evidence of overdispersion.

Table 6.1 Regression Results: Aggregate Top Public Laws

	Top 3,500		Top 500	
Polarization measure				
Aggregate	−0.828***		−0.961**	
	(0.228)		(0.404)	
DW-NOMINATE		−0.759**		−1.037*
		(0.369)		(0.603)
Control variables				
Start of term	0.196***	0.183**	0.425***	0.412***
	(0.0757)	(0.0815)	(0.133)	(0.133)
Divided government	−0.0836	−0.0844	−0.264*	−0.253*
	(0.0793)	(0.0853)	(0.141)	(0.142)
War	0.122	0.145	0.183	0.187
	(0.118)	(0.130)	(0.199)	(0.207)
Vietnam War	0.145	0.334**	0.357	0.565***
	(0.138)	(0.132)	(0.228)	(0.203)
Time	0.0272***	0.0244***	0.00866**	0.00447
	(0.00249)	(0.00348)	(0.00440)	(0.00564)
House majority party advantage	0.171	0.137	1.044**	0.976*
	(0.315)	(0.344)	(0.518)	(0.535)
Constant	4.297***	3.567***	2.912***	2.197***
	(0.396)	(0.341)	(0.707)	(0.559)
Observations	59	59	59	59
Alpha	0.0544	0.0664	0.0957	0.0989

Note: Standard errors in parentheses.
*** $p < 0.01$; ** $p < 0.05$; * $p < 0.1$

finding is that it does not matter much whether one uses a DW-NOMINATE or the aggregate mean Bayesian measure of polarization introduced in chapter 4.[10] Now I turn to what is specifically shown in the aggregate models.

[10] The aggregate polarization finding reported in this chapter is not robust if I do not use the aggregate mean–adjusted ideal points. In other words, if I substitute the Bayesian-generated ideal points using all roll call votes that are adjusted by the Groseclose et al. (1999) method reported in chapter 3 that are not a mean average, the findings are substantively different. At the aggregate

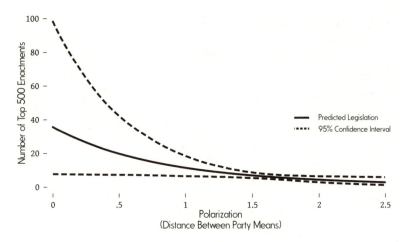

Figure 6.1
Predicted Top 500 Enactments (Aggregate)

An assessment of the measures based on the effects on the top 500 significant enactments finds that political polarization depresses lawmaking activity at a significant level.[11] The other important determinants of legislative productivity for the top 500 landmark laws is start of term, size of the majority party, the Vietnam War indicator, and divided government. The start-of-term variable, which measures whether or not a Congress is the first of a presidential term, is positive and statistically significant. Divided government depresses legislative productivity for the top 500 laws, but this finding does not hold when we turn to a study of the top 3,500 laws.

In order to substantively interpret the results of the top-500 model, figure 6.1 calculates out how the amount of legislative productivity changes as we vary the level of polarization. In computing these effects, other continuous variables are held at their means, and indicator variables, including start of term, divided government, war, and Vietnam War, are held at 0. Figure 6.1 shows that as we vary political polarization there are large changes to legislative productivity. This is not a surprising finding, as similar results have been shown by others (Lapinski 2008; McCarty, Poole, and Rosenthal 2006). The figure shows the range as political polarization is varied. Substantively, if we

---

level, polarization is no longer statistically significant. As reported earlier, this finding will be explored in more detail at a later date with my colleague Joshua Clinton.

[11] This is true whether one uses the overall aggregate measure of polarization introduced in chapter 3 or a DW-NOMINATE-based measure of polarization. In discussing the results for the models analyzing all top 500 and top 3,500 enactments, I focus only on my measure of aggregate polarization, as the results are very similar to the DW-NOMINATE results.

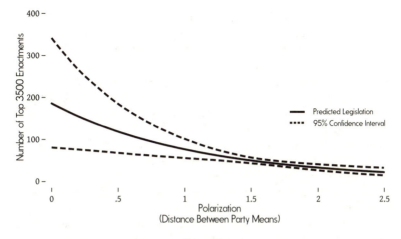

Figure 6.2
Predicted Top 3,500 Enactments (Aggregate)

were to set polarization at its mean, we would observe around six (6.4) top 500 laws. If we increase polarization by one standard deviation, we would observe four and a half (4.51) top 500 laws. This represents a decrease of 29 percent.

Of course, political polarization is not the only important determinant of significant lawmaking. Start of term also has a large and important effect on this type of lawmaking. If we are in a start-of-term Congress, we would expect to see just under ten (9.73) laws produced, in contrast to around six (6.42) top 500 enactments in a non-first term. This represents a change of 51 percent. This effect is huge, though not necessarily surprising.

The size of the majority party is also an important factor in top-500 law-making. The larger the size of the majority, the more legislatively productive the Congress is. If we change the size of the majority party by one standard deviation from its mean, we observe a 14 percent increase in productivity. Contra Mayhew's (1991) finding, divided government suppresses lawmaking by one and a half (1.53) laws, which represents a 24 percent decrease.

The model for the top 3,500 enactments shows results similar to those for the top-500 models, except that divided government is no longer statistically significant. Political polarization is a significant factor in determining the number of important enactments produced. Here we observe forty-seven (46.55) laws if polarization is set at its mean, compared to thirty-four (34.16) laws if we increase polarization by one standard deviation. This represent a nontrivial decrease of 27 percent. Figure 6.2 plots the predicted probabilities as polarization varies. Start of term also is an important factor for top-3,500 legislative productivity, though the effect is muted in comparison to top-500 lawmaking. In a first term, we would observe an additional ten laws, which represents approximately a 22 percent increase from a non-first-term Congress. A larger majority also leads to an increase in significant legislation.

Overall, the aggregate-level analyses of the top 500 and top 3,500 sets of laws provide confirming evidence for the findings of the bulk of scholarly work on this topic. A notable exception is the divided-government finding. However, these results do nothing to answer the question of whether overall lawmaking behaves in a similar way by policy issue area. In order to answer this question, we must assess lawmaking across different issue areas. Another important question must be examined: Does measuring political preferences by issue area give us additional analytical leverage in understanding the policymaking process? I next turn to these questions.

Tables 6.2 through 6.5 provide the multivariate results broken down by laws in the tier 1 issue areas using the thresholds of top-500 and top-3,500 measures of legislative productivity described in chapter 5. Each tier 1 category by significance threshold has two associated models. The first model always contains the results using the issue-specific measure of polarization developed in this book, while the second column uses a DW-NOMINATE aggregate measure of polarization. The two models are presented to illustrate the cost of relying on non-issue-specific measures of polarization.

Table 6.2 provides the multivariate analyses for sovereignty policy. The models for sovereignty policy diverge considerably from overall lawmaking as well as from lawmaking in the other tier 1 categories. The most striking finding for the sovereignty models is that the sign for the political polarization measures is in an unexpected direction and is statistically significant for both of the top-3,500 models. The only other significant variable in the top-3,500 models is the Vietnam War variable. These results provide strong evidence that sovereignty lawmaking is quite dissimilar from other issue areas. Clearly, the most intriguing finding in these models is that increased polarization leads to more sovereignty policy. It is also notable that other variables, such as start of term, size of the majority party, and divided government, have no significant effect on productivity.

A plausible explanation for these findings arose in chapter 4, where the qualitative casework showed that intraparty conflict often characterizes sovereignty policy. This conflict is also often regionally based: southern and northern Democrats were pitted against each other during the civil rights era, and during the early part of the twentieth century intraparty splits were common among Republicans. In any case, it is clearly the case that policymaking behavior is drastically different for sovereignty policy than for other issue areas.

Lawmaking in the domain of organization and scope policy also behaves in a way quite different from the behavior of overall lawmaking. Table 6.3 provides the multivariate results for this issue area. None of the covariates, except time, are statistically significant. There is a different picture for

Table 6.2 Regression Results: Sovereignty Public Laws

	Top 3,500		Top 500	
Polarization measures				
Sovereignty	0.547***		0.251	
	(0.195)		(0.410)	
DW-NOMINATE		2.426***		1.422
		(0.676)		(1.442)
Control variables				
Start of term	0.128	0.146	0.349	0.348
	(0.148)	(0.148)	(0.312)	(0.309)
Divided government	−0.116	−0.0794	−0.231	−0.213
	(0.151)	(0.150)	(0.322)	(0.320)
War	0.316	0.256	0.133	0.144
	(0.248)	(0.229)	(0.520)	(0.478)
Vietnam War	0.437*	0.424*	0.794*	0.816*
	(0.250)	(0.242)	(0.474)	(0.462)
Time	0.00479	0.0129**	−0.00183	0.00350
	(0.00465)	(0.00579)	(0.0108)	(0.0129)
House majority party advantage	−0.750	−0.437	−0.886	−0.702
	(0.621)	(0.637)	(1.303)	(1.330)
Constant	0.519	−0.796	−0.503	−1.368
	(0.344)	(0.626)	(0.737)	(1.331)
Observations	59	59	59	59
Alpha	0	0	1.13e-06	9.88e-07

Note: Standard errors in parentheses.
*** $p < 0.01$; ** $p < 0.05$; * $p < 0.1$

top-3,500 models of lawmaking. This is an example of the need to have an issue-specific measure of polarization to find a statistically significant effect on lawmaking. Here we observe that an increase of one standard deviation of the issue-specific measure leads to a 14 percent decrease in productivity. The models of top-3,500 lawmaking also show that there is significantly more legislation during a presidential first term. Substantively, we observe a 48.6 percent increase of organization and scope laws during a presidential first term. Of course, this represents a net change of about one and a half laws, as we

Table 6.3 Regression Results: Organization and Scope Public Laws

	Top 3,500		Top 500	
Polarization measures				
Organization and scope	−0.996*		-1.711	
	(0.567)		(1.583)	
DW-NOMINATE		−0.444		-1.856
		(0.751)		(1.771)
Control variables				
Start of term	0.410**	0.382**	0.165	0.147
	(0.162)	(0.163)	(0.381)	(0.379)
Divided government	−0.160	−0.198	−0.178	−0.225
	(0.175)	(0.175)	(0.385)	(0.386)
War	−0.0401	0.00273	−0.0357	−0.111
	(0.242)	(0.260)	(0.557)	(0.584)
Vietnam War	0.0507	0.192	0.286	0.387
	(0.258)	(0.247)	(0.683)	(0.671)
Time	0.0186***	0.0127*	−0.0180	−0.0308*
	(0.00570)	(0.00668)	(0.0134)	(0.0176)
House majority party advantage	−0.490	−0.458	−1.396	−1.571
	(0.677)	(0.698)	(1.542)	(1.577)
Constant	2.156**	1.090	2.906	1.919
	(0.854)	(0.686)	(2.469)	(1.612)
Observations	59	59	59	59
Alpha	0.0578	0.0626	0.289	0.299

Note: Standard errors in parentheses.
*** $p < 0.01$; ** $p < 0.05$; * $p < 0.1$

expect about three (2.95) laws in a non-first-term Congress to around four and a half (4.4) in a first term. Still, this is a very big increase.

International affairs scholars have shown that policymaking within this realm behaves differently than domestic politics (Carroll 1958; Westerfield 1955; Gowa 1998; Howell and Pevehouse 2005). The empirical analyses shown in table 6.4 confirm this idea. A stark finding in this table is related to the effect of war on lawmaking. War is only significant for international affairs issues. This is a clear instance in which the pooling of all tier 1 categories is

Table 6.4 Regression Results: International Relations Public Laws

	Top 3,500		Top 500	
Polarization measures				
International relations	−0.461***		−0.154	
	(0.169)		(0.406)	
DW-NOMINATE		−0.510		−0.995
		(0.471)		(0.998)
Control variables				
Start of term	0.0781	0.0630	0.623**	0.654***
	(0.0967)	(0.103)	(0.249)	(0.250)
Divided government	−0.144	−0.111	−0.209	−0.174
	(0.105)	(0.111)	(0.266)	(0.269)
War	0.539***	0.564***	0.865***	0.766***
	(0.140)	(0.158)	(0.276)	(0.296)
Vietnam War	0.0532	0.206	−1.471**	−1.468**
	(0.159)	(0.156)	(0.748)	(0.733)
Time	0.0240***	0.0241***	0.00335	−0.00194
	(0.00340)	(0.00446)	(0.00790)	(0.00975)
House majority party advantage	0.155	0.198	0.883	0.718
	(0.422)	(0.449)	(0.890)	(0.900)
Constant	2.272***	1.940***	−0.0681	0.540
	(0.319)	(0.434)	(0.780)	(0.938)
Observations	59	59	59	59
Alpha	0.0411	0.0553	1.68e-06	5.79e-07

Note: Standard errors in parentheses.
*** $p < 0.01$; ** $p < 0.05$; * $p < 0.1$

highly consequential because war would not significantly affect policy if the categories were not disaggregated. The effect of war on top-500 lawmaking is an extra law passed (2.08) for every one law passed without its presence. This represents a doubling of output. Another important finding is that political polarization significantly depresses lawmaking for the top 3,500, but only if a measure of polarization for IR policy is used. The effect is very large. If polarization is increased by one standard deviation, we observe a decrease of over two laws (21 percent). Using the DW-NOMINATE measure would

Table 6.5 Regression Results: Domestic Politics Public Laws

	Top 3,500		Top 500	
Polarization measures				
Domestic politics	-0.607		-0.608	
	(0.374)		(0.544)	
DW-NOMINATE		−1.423***		−1.371**
		(0.432)		(0.699)
Control variables				
Start of term	0.176*	0.205**	0.384**	0.410***
	(0.102)	(0.0943)	(0.151)	(0.146)
Divided government	−0.0821	−0.0165	−0.382**	−0.321**
	(0.109)	(0.0996)	(0.169)	(0.162)
War	0.124	0.00456	0.0746	−0.0678
	(0.160)	(0.154)	(0.240)	(0.249)
Vietnam War	0.343*	0.389***	0.743***	0.773***
	(0.182)	(0.149)	(0.243)	(0.206)
Time	0.0362***	0.0272***	0.0176***	0.00931
	(0.00346)	(0.00401)	(0.00507)	(0.00633)
House majority party advantage	0.549	0.349	1.721***	1.466**
	(0.417)	(0.397)	(0.587)	(0.590)
Constant	3.079***	3.317***	1.498	1.702***
	(0.632)	(0.397)	(0.918)	(0.649)
Observations	59	59	59	59
Alpha	0.102	0.0816	0.0922	0.0731

Note: Standard errors in parentheses.
*** $p < 0.01$; ** $p < 0.05$; * $p < 0.1$

lead one to mistakenly believe that polarization does not affect lawmaking within this domain. Figure 6.3 provides a graphical portrait of the effect of polarization on top-3,500 lawmaking with and without the presence of war. The effects of war are large and when combined with increases in political polarization have a huge impact on foreign policymaking.

The analyses of domestic policymaking are striking. Especially important is the finding that the issue-specific measures of polarization do not show a statistically significant effect. It is true that the polarization measure is signed

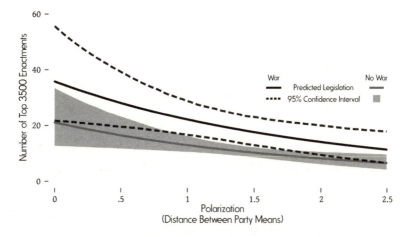

Figure 6.3
Predicted Top 3,500 Enactments (International Relations)

correctly, but this finding parallels the results reported in chapter 4 that polarization is often high in domestic politics. Divided government, however, does depress lawmaking for top-500 lawmaking in this issue domain. In fact, the presence of divided government reduced landmark lawmaking by 24 percent. Start of term led a large increase in productivity across the top-500 and top-3,500 thresholds. In the top-500 models, the increase for an increase of one standard deviation for size of majority was a 25 percent increase in domestic legislative productivity. In the top 3,500, we observe a more modest increase of 8 percent.

CONCLUSION

These results make it clear that anyone who wishes to empirically understand how lawmaking operates must take seriously the idea that policy substance matters. The analyses here have shown that pooling all legislation sometimes provides inaccurate portraits of how key determinants of lawmaking work. Although it has not been my goal in this chapter to fully understand all of these puzzles, I have certainly hoped to identify them by showing that a different and better empirical understanding of lawmaking is to be found in disaggregating policy and constructing appropriate, policy-specific measures of legislative accomplishment.

I also show that correctly measuring concepts like polarization by issue area leads to very different substantive conclusions about how this important variable affects legislative productivity.

Chapter VII

At the Crossroads: Policy Issue Substance, Congress, and American Political Development

NEGLECTING THE DIRECT STUDY of policy issue substance has unnecessarily weakened and stunted progress in the research programs of Congress and American political development. Of course, there are reasons why the role of policy substance in lawmaking has been omitted from these important areas of American politics. The barriers for Congress scholars primarily come from the past. Pivotal figures like Theodore Lowi and Aage Claussen demonstrated that deriving a theoretical or even empirical account of how lawmaking varies by issue area is no easy task. Other scholars, like Keith Poole and Howard Rosenthal, provided evidence that such work might be empirically unnecessary. Additionally, Congress scholars generally prefer to engage in what is referred to as "normal science"—making steady but incremental progress the goal, instead of chasing big and potentially intractable ideas. Policy issue substance is unquestionably a big idea, but I hope I have demonstrated here that it is possible to pursue big ideas while still making solid, incremental progress in understanding lawmaking and political behavior.

APD scholars have also been uninvolved in the systematic study of policy substance, and in many ways this disengagement is more puzzling, if only because the subfield would seem to have so much to gain by bringing Congress and the study of policy issue substance front and center. Why have APD scholars avoided Congress? It would appear that their concerns about constancy of models, generalizations, and behavior across time have led them to shy away from becoming directly engaged with the study of Congress and thus issue substance and lawmaking. This is a pity, because APD could contribute much to this area of study by helping to show how historical contingency matters as well as when model portability hurts rather than helps our understanding of a Congress-centered policy process.

The connective tissue to bring APD into the fold of Congress studies is policy issue substance. The coding schema and data introduced and deployed in this book provide a path that could lead APD in this direction.

The book has also provided Congress scholars with much-needed refined measures of political preferences as well as direct measures of legislative productivity. All of the data constructed in this book, including the lawmaking data set and measures of political preferences, are available for download at www.polisci.upenn.edu/~lapins/. The hope is that this schema can provide a uniform standard for political scientists. By "standard" I mean that it is no longer necessary to derive new coding schemas for laws and roll calls. Instead, scholars can parse and combine this flexible template as they like.[1] This type of standard will allow scholars to replicate work more easily, and will also allow for simpler comparisons across studies.

The goal of the remainder of this chapter is to show how policy issue substance can positively influence research in two important subfields of American politics, American political development and congressional studies, though I put more emphasis on APD. Each of these subfields has had difficulty in keeping up with its past success. The simple explanation is that all of the low-hanging fruit has been picked, leading scholars in each field to take different directions. Several APD scholars, for instance, have stopped focusing on core issues dealing with development and dispersed their energy on a wide range of topics and questions, thus contributing to an identity problem for APD. This is at least the conclusion reached by Karen Orren and Stephen Skowronek—two influential scholars who helped define American political development as a subfield through their research as well as their vision in creating the subfield's premier journal, *Studies in American Political Development*—in their book *The Search for American Political Development* (2004). Orren and Skowronek argue that APD's biggest hurdle is to reestablish itself as a relevant and important subfield in American politics by redefining its identity. In short, they believe that APD is facing a critical juncture where it must either reinvent itself to remain a distinct subfield or see itself be folded into other subfields within American politics or disciplines, like history. Although Orren and Skowronek's book is thought-provoking, in my opinion it does not provide concrete guidance to APD scholars for achieving this goal. The coding schema and data presented in this book provide a tangible approach for APD scholars to study policy making while still being guided by the core ideas developed by their subfield over the past three decades.

Congress scholars face a similar crossroads. As mentioned earlier, students of Congress understand what they want to accomplish—essentially, to understand why members of Congress behave as they do, and how the policymaking process works. The problem is that these questions have been answered as well as possible at the aggregate level. Congress scholars have learned most

---

[1] The data will be readily available, and the American Institutions Project, codirected by Ira Katznelson and myself, will keep the data updated.

of what they can from the existing data used to assess such questions.[2] We do not know, however, whether what we have found at the aggregate level holds across different disaggregated issue areas. Consequently, Congress scholars could benefit greatly from disaggregating lawmaking and political behavior by policy issue substance. The next two sections offer ideas for each subfield on revitalizing itself by drawing on policy issue substance.

IDEAS FOR AMERICAN POLITICAL DEVELOPMENT

Congress has been situated on the periphery of the subfield of American political development despite the institution's centrality to the political history of the United States and to political science as a discipline.[3] Keith Whittington (1999, 44) was one of the first scholars to recognize this: "Scholars in the American Political Development tradition have never fully integrated Congress, as they have other important institutions such as the bureaucracy, the presidency, political parties and the courts." But is the neglect of Congress costly? This seems to be the more important question for APD.

As I have argued elsewhere, neglecting Congress has weakened APD unnecessarily and stunted its important research program on liberalism, periodization, state building, and policy feedback. All of these research programs could be enhanced—and in some cases revived—through examining Congress with a focus on policy issue substance within the institution. In this section I briefly focus on some accomplishments of APD, then home in on two core programs: liberalism and periodization. I also discuss how and why it would be useful to include the study of Congress, and particularly the study of policy substance in Congress, in these two areas of study, which I chose because they have the greatest potential to create cross-fertilization between the Congress and APD subfields.

Nearly all practitioners of APD would agree that APD is interested in political change with a focus on "how past and present politics are connected, [and] by what bridges and processes" (Orren and Skowronek 2004, 4). To this end, APD scholars have worked primarily in four genres. Some explore critical periods through simplification, that is, by highlighting a small number of factors that they hypothesize to be critical and treating them analytically and causally. This is what Stephen Skowronek (1982), has accomplished for

---

[2] A constant lament during Congress panels at professional meetings is that fresh approaches are needed to refresh the subfield. There are many complaints that too much emphasis is put on conducting large-N roll call analyses and not enough on politics. Calls are often made to "fix" this problem by doing case studies of particular policies or committees and conducting more qualitative research, particularly interviews of elites such as legislators and their staffers.

[3] This section has been excerpted and adapted from Katznelson and Lapinski (2006a).

progressivism, Richard Bensel (1990) for the Civil War and Reconstruction as well as the Gilded Age (Bensel 2000), Gretchen Ritter (1997) and Elizabeth Sanders (1999) for populism, and David Plotke (1996) for the New Deal. Others steer a critical subject through key moments or even the whole of American history. In this manner, Desmond King (1995), Rogers Smith (1997), Daniel Kryder (2000), and Richard Valelly (2004) have probed race and membership; Dan Tichenor (2002) and Aristide Zolberg (2006; Zolberg and Benda 2001) have illuminated immigration; Marie Gottschalk (2000), Jacob Hacker (2002), and Theda Skocpol (1996) have clarified the history and dynamics of social policy; and Amy Bridges (1997) and Victoria Hattam (1993) have examined working-class formation. A third vein, including Skowronek's (1997) work on the presidency, Eric Schickler's writing on Congress (2001), and Daniel Carpenter's on the executive branch (2001), traces the development of key institutions in the medium and long term. Finally, there is a sizable body of APD writing on political speech and ideas that includes important contributions by J. David Greenstone (1993) and Eldon Eisenach (1994).

American political development's practitioners have returned again and again to a small number of vital substantive themes, especially the character, contours, and limits of the liberal political tradition and the qualities of the national state. Reviving and advancing an intellectual conversation pioneered in the 1950s (Hartz 1955), they have asked which political ideas and ideologies, especially those associated with the Western liberal tradition, have shaped the development of the American regime. Associated with the effort to "bring the state back in" (Evans, Rueschemeyer, and Skocpol 1985; Tilly 1975), they also have sought to understand how the national government, despite very modest beginnings, developed as a modern national state. Intent on understanding not only what government is but what it does, they have probed the reciprocal links that connect politics to policy (Pierson 1994; Skocpol 1992), the relationship of ideas and interests (Lieberman 2002; Orren and Skowronek 2004), the impact of sequencing and path dependence (Pierson 2000), configurations of causal processes (Katznelson 1997; Pierson and Skocpol 2002), and the sources of preferences when situated historically (Katznelson 2003). To probe the conjunction of liberalism and the state, APD has stressed the importance of systematic approaches to temporality, including distinctions between "critical junctures" and more normal periods and the mechanism of policy feedback.

Even though it is still young, American political development can boast many advances in these areas. Orren and Skowronek (2004) argue forcefully, however, that APD needs to refocus in order to remain coherent as a subfield and help secure and extend the tradition's core intellectual attainments. I largely agree with their assessment and would argue that policy issue substance and the study of Congress are the keys to accomplishing their goal. For APD, a compelling return to the substance of lawmaking is essential to making Congress a constitutive feature of analyses of the most pressing questions on its own research agenda. But this restoration will not succeed unless it can overcome the main bottlenecks that have stymied this enterprise in the past: the absence of theoretically grounded and empirically useful classifications of legislative content. With such substantive tools, APD could undertake a confident conversation with recent theory building and empirical scholarship by students of Congress, make connections with these literatures that are consistent with its own larger purposes, and move the center of gravity of congressional scholarship closer to its own big themes.

The gains produced by a more Congress-oriented APD thus might pay dividends in more than one place. A preview of how policy substance can help advance the understanding of temporality and liberalism follows.

Temporality

As a first example, consider how APD's stress on temporality has been inhibited by the relatively modest notice it has given to Congress. The main hinge of APD work on periodization was first provided by studies of electoral behavior that demarcated distinctive party systems based on oscillations of electoral stability and change. Seeking to extend the scholarship of V. O. Key (1955) on critical elections, Walter Dean Burnham (1970) used the theme of electoral realignments as the main mechanism by which an unchanging regime can accommodate environmental transformations. As the world changes, so do the pressures brought to bear on politics. When existing party alignments do not accommodate them, he argued, political entrepreneurs emerge who, by introducing new issues into the political arena, force a realignment of partisan forces. American history could thus be divided, he hypothesized, into electoral phases. Inevitably, such work entailed an understanding of more than elections and partisanship because it addressed the big questions of institutions, norms, and behavior that are central to APD.

Once scholars in this tradition began to think about periodization as a concern with critical junctures marked by large-scale changes rather than by a study of electoral transformations (Collier and Collier 1991), about which there are good grounds for unease (Mayhew 2002), the subject of temporality emerged for even richer explorations. There may not be one master temporal dynamic, but rather multiple patterns that are characteristic of different institutional realms (Orren and Skowronek 1994). Slow-moving processes may intersect with swift-moving developments to produce relatively open historical conjunctures (Shefter 1977), and different institutions moving at their own tempo can interconnect to produce key outcomes that each, on its own, might not. Thus, just as the dynamics of the presidency may differ from those of the

Supreme Court, or the private sector from the public, it is the combination of their temporalities that often produces key outcomes (Hacker 2002; James 2000; Skowronek 1997). Further, policy legacies from times past can shape and constrain future possibilities (Finegold and Skocpol 1995; Katznelson 1981; Pierson 1993; Weir 1992).

Issues of periodization and temporality, in short, are rich, vexing, and complicated. This is all the more reason not to set aside the massive body of evidence offered by congressional debates and decisions about preferences and policies. If, for example, as Jerome Clubb, William Flanigan, and Nancy Zingale (1980) have argued, enduring partisan change comes about only when "critical election" voting results are quickly followed by policy changes that secure the realignment and cause it to persist by offering continuing incentives to the new majority coalition of voters, then charting changes to policymaking becomes a central task (Brady 1988; Mayhew 2002). The legislative performance data in this book could be fruitfully used to test such a proposition. More importantly, these data provide the opportunity to determine if certain types of policies are more likely to occur after a critical election. APD is well poised to examine these types of ideas with the detail they deserve.

Among other possibilities, the scrutiny of congressional behavior makes available a critical body of evidence about other subjects of keen interest to APD. Have temporal shifts occurred? What is their content? How are partisanship and policy substance connected? Of the relevant structural features that influence behavior and performance, which are malleable and endogenous? How are changes within the congressional arena linked to other institutional settings? One of the more promising points of intellectual contact lies in an area central to APD: understanding how institutions evolve and affect policymaking (as distinct from behavioral variables that predict policy outcomes). This phenomenon is very important to congressional scholars, who have entered into a robust conversation about explanations for the emergence of rules in both the House and the Senate that enhance or detract from partisan objectives. For example, Eric Schickler (2001) has examined rule changes in the House of Representatives that are partisan in nature. He tests competing explanations: an "ideological balance of power" model (that is, a median voter–based theory) versus "conditional party government" theory (Binder 1996; Rohde 1991), a "majority party cartel" model (Cox and McCubbins 1993, 2005), and a "pivotal politics" model (Krehbiel 1998). The participants in this conversation are interested in how rules in Congress, primarily in the House, evolve over time. This interest is motivated by the profound impact that congressional rules can have on the policymaking process. For example, Gary Cox and Matthew McCubbins's party cartel model applies only to the post–"Reed's rules" Congresses, and Keith Krehbiel's pivotal politics model applies only after the Senate adopted Rule XXII in 1917, formally establishing cloture. Changes in rules, moreover, often are associated with forces outside Congress and thus can help trace both the impact of larger temporal dynamics on Congress and the impact of shifts inside the institution on larger political phenomena. By identifying and parsing such temporal orders from a congressional vantage, especially those that revolve around partisanship, APD would bring greater depth to reexaminations of its prevailing judgments about periodization. This can now be done with the political preference data introduced in chapter 3, parsed by substantive policy issue areas. This splitting can also be done at different levels of aggregation via the tiers in the schema presented in this book. All of this has the potential to provide a fresh cut at examining periodization.

Liberalism

American political development's focus on the status of liberalism has been characterized by a continuing—perhaps compulsive—engagement with a text: Louis Hartz's extended essay on *The Liberal Tradition in America* (1955), published well before ADP emerged in the early 1980s as a distinct subfield. Claiming that liberalism has been the most important underlying force in American history, Hartz famously argued that its standing and power were constituted by the non-appearance of feudalism on American soil. Lacking an adversary, the contractual, individualist, and constitutional liberalism identified most closely with John Locke gained free sway in the United States and quickly came to possess the power to snuff out either pre- or anti-liberal impulses of various kinds. Though hardly a celebrant of these qualities, Hartz claimed that meaningful stories about the American regime must be contained inside the boundaries of the exceptional history that has flattened the country's politics to this single dimension, as both "left" and "right" are contained within a common liberal world, a world of one regime and one big ideology that has defined the poles of partisan politics.

Was Hartz right? Has a single tradition aligning and confining American politics within a single dimension that divides one kind of political liberal from another been the main hallmark of political thought and practice? (On this reading, conservatives in the American lexicon are a particular kind of liberal.) Much of APD has tried to figure out the standing of what Hartz (1955, 10–11) called "the moral unanimity" of the country's "nationalist articulation of Locke."

It is possible to identify two discrete positions regarding this claim. The first has been to discover sources of diversity and thus of change contained within a persistent and encompassing liberal political culture. As a leading instance, and borrowing from Wittgenstein, David Greenstone's *The Lincoln Persuasion* (1993, 42, 45) reread Hartz's unidimensional claim not as one that defines the end of conflict but as one that recognizes relatively fixed norms of speech and action that define what he calls a boundary condition, "a set of relatively permanent features of a particular context that affect causal relationships within it," even as that context remains subject to dispute. Much as institutions can make some moves possible and others impossible within a given set of rules, liberalism as a capacious but circumscribed set of ideas makes some cognitions and behavior "natural" while relegating other forms of thought and conduct to the zone of the not-imagined and not-done. From this revised Hartzian perspective, to say that liberalism has been overriding is not the same as to argue that it has been uniform or unchanging.

A second position, forcefully advanced by Rogers Smith (1993, 1997), argues that American politics has not been characterized or contained by a single liberal dimension but rather by multiple traditions, especially those he has identified as liberalism, republicanism, and ascriptive forms of Americanism, especially racism. "At its heart," he has written, "the multiple-traditions thesis holds that the definitive feature of American political culture has been not its liberal, republican, or 'ascriptive-Americanist' elements, but, rather, [a] more complex pattern of apparently inconsistent combinations of the traditions, accompanied by recurring conflicts" (Smith 1993, 558). On this view, in short, politics in the United States has been conducted in more than one dominant dimension. In collaboration with King, Smith has expanded on this idea to show that American politics might be studied by using a framework that classifies American political history as being captured by the dimensions they call a "white supremacist order" and an "egalitarian transformative order" (King and Smith 2005).[4]

Hartz styled his book as a work of political theory. APD's line of writing about the status of the Western liberal tradition also has proceeded for the most part at the level of the history of political thought, including its articulation in jurisprudence. Greenstone was concerned primarily with the poles of rhetoric deployed within debates about slavery. Smith built his critique of Hartz mainly on a massive body of the discourse in court decisions concerning laws about citizenship.

Generously put, none of APD's influential works about the liberal tradition foreground Congress. This is a good deal more than a casual observation, for Congress offers scholars four sets of evidence, all of which are germane to the long-standing quest to make sense of the status of liberalism in America. The record of its deliberations, kept for more than two centuries, presents a remarkable compilation of discourse by political representatives. Less systematic than the considered prose of senior judges but more focused and learned than most mass journalism or popular discussion, this archive of speech is

---

[4] King and Smith (2005) make the case that studying Congress using this framework would be a very useful exercise.

vastly underexploited. Second, there is the development of Congress as an institution, one that acts for and gives meaning to political representation by inviting citizens to signify by various means what they would like legislators to do and by providing the means for legislators who receive such signals to subject them to critical evaluation and reach authoritative decisions. Congress has also been a site of regular, ritualized, and recorded political behavior. Thus, the third type of evidence is found in the many studies of roll call voting, but precious few scholars have self-consciously linked this fantastic archive to the liberalism question—or, for that matter, to APD's other themes of state building and policy feedback. Finally, Congress proffers a body of information in the statutes it has created. Here, both the outlines and details of public policy express and shape the character of the state's public philosophy. The last two sets of evidence are used in this book to create measures for empirical testing purposes.

But here lies the rub. From the side of theorists like Hartz, Greenstone, and Smith, there is no systematic empirical work on congressional behavior. This is distressful not for any general principle that political theory should be linked to empirical observation, although that is usually a good idea. It is distressful because the most original and central pivot of the liberal tradition is political representation based on consent, which is a critical institutional means not only to place the preferences of civil society within the state but to prevent tyranny (Manin 1997; Przeworski, Stokes, and Manin 1999).

The political preference data and the lawmaking data split by policy issue areas provide excellent tools for assessing the liberalism question. I would argue that what we are really considering here is not how many "dimensions" exist in American politics at particular moments in time, but instead how preferences vary across different distinct issue areas. Consider the case studies provided in chapter 4. They provide a quick glance at how ascriptive ideas are present in particular moments of policymaking. They show this by issue area, and they also present the opportunity to study particular groups of legislators. For example, we may want to know when and for what issues key geographic groups like southern Democrats act on Hartzian terms and when they demonstrate more ascriptive attitudes. Surely, when one considers Smith's challenge to Hartz as an important instance, it would be at least as noteworthy as the study of deliberation in the courts to consider how Congress has undertaken in debate and behavior the task of defining the properties, contours, limits, and advances of American liberalism. After all, it has been in Congress, where legislative compromise almost always is necessary, that historically specific resolutions to the complex and variable relationship between liberalism and racism have been crafted within the framework of congressional representation. This type of analysis will help these literatures be more than only partially realized.

IDEAS FOR CONGRESSIONAL STUDIES

In a provocative essay, Lisa Anderson, president of the American University in Cairo, argues that political scientists must change their ways in order to stay relevant in today's world. She writes in her abstract:

> This article argues that the technological structure of the modern world has reshaped drastically the role of political scientists as purveyors of information. Only a few decades ago, scholars were still central to the development, collection and dissemination of knowledge. But the transformation in the availability of data due to the proliferation of social media and research engines creates a new environment in which scholars can no longer claim to be erudite carriers of hard-to-get facts. (Anderson 2012, 385)

Anderson is correct that political scientists must be adaptive to remain relevant; however, she is not quite right in her thinking about the role of political scientists in creating data. To be fair, her focus is outside of American politics, with more of an eye on students of foreign affairs. So perhaps she is writing about a particular subset of political scientists, though she does not make this distinction in her article. That said, she confuses data and measurement. This is a distinction that students of American politics understand well. Data are often useless unless they are properly transformed into useful measures to help us better understand political processes. Political scientists still have a very important role in providing data and better measurement to understand political phenomena. In a way, this book is all about measurement. And I think the measures introduced here have the potential to help Congress scholars immensely as well as pundits interested in this institution.

My ideas for improving congressional studies are all about introducing better measures of political preferences and legislative productivity. I believe that providing good measures, not more theory, is what is needed to revive congressional studies. Much of what can be done with better measures has been previewed in this book. In particular, I think that better measurement enables us to assess our theoretical accounts of lawmaking in a much more satisfying manner, as well as explore topics like political polarization in a more sophisticated way. In addition, better measurement gives us more opportunities to study fresh topics, including political entrepreneurs, via policy issue substance.

The political preference data in this book provides us with the opportunity to determine who is pivotal in Congress. The casework provides extensive evidence that who is pivotal depends on the policy area considered. Determining who is pivotal in American politics is critical for literally all modern theories of lawmaking. The case studies in chapter 4 show that there is tremendous variation across pivotal players—whether we are looking at median members in the House, key members in the pivotal politics theory of lawmaking, or party-based theories. Using aggregate-level measures like NOMINATE misses the mark for many policy areas. In order to really understand how lawmaking works, we must correctly identify the key political actors. In fact, I think this is a critical area of study for Congress scholars. The political preference data in this book allow for this. This type of data might provide the evidence necessary to finally come to a better conclusion on whether party versus pivotal politics models better explain lawmaking. Alternatively, a simple median voter model may have more explanatory power. In order to answer these questions, we need better and more refined measures of the political preferences of members of Congress. This book provides the framework and data needed for this task.

The preference data also can be used to better understand political polarization. Chapter 3 begins to unpack how polarization behaves across issue areas but, of course, only scratches the surface of this question. It is a question of the utmost importance. If the analyses in chapter 3 withstand the scrutiny of other scholars, Congress scholars will need a theoretical account of why such issues as sovereignty and international affairs issues vary so much in terms of polarization and other issues do not. This book does provide empirical generalizations and some ideas about this topic, particularly in regard to sovereignty issues, but much more is needed here. The Congress subfield is well suited to filling this void.

Studying legislative productivity by policy issue area is another potentially fertile ground for Congress scholars. Clearly, explanations of lawmaking across different issue areas vary considerably. The empirical work of chapter 5 suggests that different determinants are important across tier 1 issue areas. Congress scholars are well poised to make theoretical and additional empirical progress in this area. For example, why is political polarization an important determinant in some areas but not others? How do events matter for lawmaking across issues? The data in this book allow political scientists to explore these types of questions in new ways.

Congressional studies and American political development are at a crossroads. Policy issue substance seems to offer a path to fruitful work that can help both fields make much-needed gains in our understanding of the policy process as well as provide key insights into long-standing but only partially answered core questions asked by each subfield. It is my hope that such work will also bring the subfields closer to each other. If this happens, this book will have served its purpose.

Bibliography

Adler, E. Scott, and John S. Lapinski. 2006. *The Macropolitics of Congress*. Princeton, NJ: Princeton University Press.

Aldrich, John. 1995. *Why Parties? The Origin and Transformation of Party Politics in America*. Chicago: University of Chicago Press.

Aldrich, John, and David Rohde. 2000. "The Consequences of Party Organization in the House: The Role of the Majority in Majority and Minority Parties in Conditional Party Government." In *Polarized Politics: Congress and the President in a Partisan Era*. Washington, DC: Congressional Quarterly Press.

Aleinikoff, T. Alexander. 2002. *Semblances of Sovereignty: The Constitution, the State, and American Citizenship*. Cambridge, MA: Harvard University Press.

Anderson, Lisa. 2012. "Too Much Information? Political Science, the University, and the Public Sphere." *Perspectives on Politics* 10(2): 385–96.

Arnold, R. Douglas. 1990. *The Logic of Congressional Action*. New Haven, CT: Yale University Press.

Baldwin, David A. 1995. "Security Studies and the End of the Cold War." *World Politics* 48(1): 117–41.

Baumgartner, Frank, and Bryan D. Jones. 1993. *Agendas and Instability in American Politics*. Chicago: University of Chicago Press.

———. 2002. *Policy Dynamics*. Chicago: University of Chicago Press.

———. 2004. "The Evolution of American Government: Information, Attention, and Policy Punctuations." Unpublished paper, Pennsylvania State University.

Baumgartner, Frank R., Bryan D. Jones, and Michael C. MacLeod. 1998. "Lessons from the Trenches: Quality, Reliability, and Usability in a New Data Source." *The Political Methodologist* 8(2): 2–10.

Bensel, Richard. 1990. *Yankee Leviathan: The Origins of Central State Authority in America, 1859–1877*. New York: Cambridge University Press.

———. 2000. *The Political Economy of American Industrialization, 1877–1900*. New York: Cambridge University Press.

Binder, Sarah. 1996. "The Partisan Basis of Procedural Choice: Allocating Parliamentary Rights in the House, 1789–1990." *American Political Science Review* 90: 8–20.

———. 1999. "The Dynamics of Legislative Gridlock, 1947–1996." *American Political Science Review* 93(3): 519–33.

———. 2003. *Causes and Consequences of Legislative Gridlock*. Washington, DC: Brookings Institution Press.

Bornet, Vaughn Davis. 1983. *The American Presidency of Lyndon B. Johnson*. Lawrence: University Press of Kansas.

Bosniak, Linda. 2006. *The Citizen and the Alien: Dilemmas of Contemporary Membership*. Princeton, NJ: Princeton University Press.

Brady, David. 1988. *Critical Elections and Congressional Policy Making*. Palo Alto, CA: Stanford University Press.

Brady, David, and Joseph Cooper. 1981. "Toward a Diachronic Analysis of Congress." *American Political Science Review* 75: 988–1006.

Brady, David, and Joseph Stewart. 1982. "Congressional Party Realignment and Transformations of Public Policy in Three Realignment Eras." *American Journal of Political Science* 26: 333–60.

Brady, David, and Craig Volden. 1998. *Revolving Gridlock*. Boulder, CO: Westview Press.

Bridges, Amy. 1997. *Morning Glories: Municipal Reform in the Southwest*. Princeton, NJ: Princeton University Press.

Buchanan, Russell A. 1964. *The United States and World War II*. 2 vols. New York: Harper & Row.

Burnham, Walter Dean. 1970. *Critical Elections and the Mainsprings of American Politics*. New York: W. W. Norton & Co.

Cameron, Charles. 2000. *Veto Bargaining: Presidents and the Politics of Negative Power*. New York: Cambridge University Press.

Cameron, Charles, John S. Lapinski, and Charles Riemann. 2000. "Testing Formal Theories of Political Rhetoric." *Journal of Politics* 62: 187–205.

Carpenter, Daniel P. 2001. *The Forging of Bureaucratic Autonomy: Reputations, Networks, and Policy Innovation in Executive Agencies, 1862–1928*. Princeton, NJ: Princeton University Press.

Carroll, Holbert. 1958. *The House of Representatives and Foreign Affairs*. Pittsburgh: University of Pittsburgh Press.

Chamberlain, Lawrence H. 1946. *The President, Congress, and Legislation*. New York: Columbia University Press.

Clausen, Aage R. 1967. "Measurement Identity in the Longitudinal Analysis of Legislative Voting." *American Political Science Review* 41(4): 1020–35.

———. 1973. *How Congressmen Decide: A Policy Focus*. New York: St. Martin's Press.

Clausen, Aage R., and Richard B. Cheney. 1970. "A Comparative Analysis of Senate and House Voting on Economic and Welfare Policy, 1953–1964." *American Political Science Review* 44(1): 138–52.

Clements, Kendrick A. 1992. *The Presidency of Woodrow Wilson*. Lawrence: University Press of Kansas.

Cleveland, Sarah H. 2002. "Powers Inherent in Sovereignty: Indians, Aliens, Territories, and the Nineteenth-Century Origins of Plenary Power over Foreign Affairs." *Texas Law Review* 81(1): 1–284.

Clinton, Joshua D., and Simon Jackman. 2009. "To Stimulate or NOMINATE? A Comparison of the Bayesian-Normal Approach to the Analysis of Roll Call Data with W-NOMINATE." *Legislative Studies Quarterly* 34(4): 593–621.

Clinton, Joshua D., Simon Jackman, and Douglas Rivers. 2004. "The Statistical Analysis of Legislative Behavior: A Unified Approach." *American Political Science Review* 98(2): 355–70.

Clinton, Joshua, and John S. Lapinski. 2006. "Measuring Legislative Accomplishment, 1877–1946." *American Journal of Political Science* 50(1): 232–49.

———. 2008. "Laws and Roll Calls in the U.S. Congress, 1891–1994." *Legislative Studies Quarterly* 33: 511–41.

Clubb, Jerome M., William H. Flanigan, and Nancy Zingale. 1980. *Partisan Realignment: Voters, Parties, and Government in American History*. Beverly Hills, CA: Sage Publications.

Coleman, John J. 1999. "Unified Government, Divided Government, and Party Responsiveness." *American Political Science Review* 93(4): 821–35.

Coletta, Paolo E. 1973. *The Presidency of William Howard Taft*. Lawrence: University Press of Kansas.

Collier, Ruth Berns, and David Collier. 1991. *Shaping the Political Arena: Critical Junctures, the Labor Movement, and Regime Dynamics in Latin America*. Princeton, NJ: Princeton University Press.

Cox, Gary, and Mathew McCubbins. 1993. *Legislative Leviathan: Party Government in the House*. Berkeley: University of California Press.

———. 2005. *Setting the Agenda: Responsible Party Government in the U.S. House of Representatives*. New York: Cambridge University Press.

Cutler, Lloyd N. 1988. "Some Reflections About Divided Government." *Presidential Studies Quarterly* 18(3): 485–92.

Dell, Christopher, and Stephen W. Stathis. 1982. *Major Acts of Congress and Treaties Approved by the Senate, 1789–1980*. Technical Report 82-156 GOV, Congressional Research Service Report. Washington, DC: U.S. Government Printing Office.

Doenecke, Justus D. 1981. *The Presidencies of James A. Garfield and Chester A. Arthur*. Lawrence: Regents Press of Kansas.

Eisenach, Eldon J. 1994. *Lost Promise of Progressivism*. Lawrence: University of Kansas Press.

Erikson, Robert S, Michael B. Mackuen, and James A. Stimson. 2002. *The Macro Polity*. New York: Cambridge University Press.

Evans, Peter B., Dietrich Rueschemeyer, and Theda Skocpol, eds. 1985. *Bringing the State Back In*. New York: Cambridge University Press.

Faulkner, Harold U. 1959. *Politics, Reform, and Expansion, 1890–1900*. New York: Harper & Row.

Fausold, Martin L. 1985. *The Presidency of Herbert C. Hoover*. Lawrence: University Press of Kansas.

Ferejohn, John A. 1974. *Pork Barrel Politics*. Palo Alto, CA: Stanford University Press.

Ferrell, Robert H. 1985. *Woodrow Wilson and World War I, 1917–1921*. New York: Harper & Row.

———. 1998. *The Presidency of Calvin Coolidge*. Lawrence: University Press of Kansas.

Finegold, Kenneth, and Theda Skocpol. 1995. *State and Party in America's New Deal*. Madison: University of Wisconsin Press.

Garratty, John A. 1968. *The New Commonwealth, 1877–1890*. New York: Harper & Row.

Giglio, James N. 1991. *The Presidency of John F. Kennedy*. Lawrence: University Press of Kansas.

Goldman, Eric F. 1960. *The Crucial Decade and After, 1945–1960*. New York: Random House.

Gormley, Jr. William T. 2007. "Public Policy Analysis: Ideas and Impacts." *Annual Review of Political Science* 10: 297–313.

Gottschalk, Marie. 2000. *The Shadow Welfare State: Labor, Business, and the Politics of Health Care in the United States*. Ithaca, NY: Cornell University Press.

Gould, Lewis L. 1980. *The Presidency of William McKinley*. Lawrence: University Press of Kansas.

———. 1991. *The Presidency of Theodore Roosevelt*. Lawrence: University Press of Kansas.

Gowa, Joannec. 1998. "Politics at the Water's Edge: Parties, Voters, and the use of Force." *International Organization* 52(2): 307–24.

Graber, Mark A. 1993. "The Nonmajoritarian Difficulty: Legislative Deference to the Judiciary." *Studies in American Political Development* 7(1): 35–73.

Greene, John Robert. 1995. *The Presidency of Gerald R. Ford*. Lawrence: University Press of Kansas.

———. 2000. *The Presidency of George Bush*. Lawrence: University Press of Kansas.

Greenstone, J. David. 1993. *The Lincoln Persuasion: Remaking American Liberalism*. Princeton, NJ: Princeton University Press.

Groseclose, Tim, Steven D. Levitt, and James M. Snyder Jr. 1999. "Comparing Interest Group Scores Across Time and Chambers: Adjusted ADA Scores for the U.S. Congress." *American Political Science Review* 93(1): 33–50.

Hacker, Jacob. 2002. *The Divided Welfare State: The Battle over Public and Private Social Benefits in the United States*. New York: Cambridge University Press.

Hall, Richard L. 1996. *Participation in Congress*. New Haven, CT: Yale University Press.

Hartz, Louis. 1955. *The Liberal Tradition in America: An Interpretation of American Political Thought Since the Revolution*. New York: Harcourt, Brace.

Hattam, Victoria. 1993. *Labor Visions and State Power: The Origins of Business Unionism in the United States*. Princeton, NJ: Princeton University Press.

Heckman, James J., and James M. Snyder Jr. 1997. "Linear Probability Models of the Demand for Attributes with an Empirical Application to Estimating the Preferences of Legislators." *RAND Journal of Economics* 28: 142–89.

Hick, John D. 1960. *Republican Ascendancy, 1921–1933*. New York: Harper & Row.

Hoogenboom, Ari. 1988. *The Presidency of Rutherford B. Hayes*. Lawrence: University Press of Kansas.

Hough, Charles M. 1918. "Law in wartime: 1917." *Harvard Law Review* 31(5): 692–701.

Howell, William, E. Scott Adler, Charles Cameron, and Charles Riemann. 2000. "Divided Government and the Legislative Productivity of Congress, 1945–1994." *Legislative Studies Quarterly* 25(2): 285–312.

Howell, William, and Joc C. Pevehouse. 2005. "Presidents, Congress, and the Use of Force." *International Organization* 59(1): 209–32.

Jackman, Simon. 2004. "What Do We Learn from Graduate Admissions Committees? A Multiple-Rater, Latent Variable Model with Incomplete Discrete and Continuous Indicators." *Political Analysis* 12(4): 400–24.

James, Scott. 2000. *Parties, Presidents, and the State: Electoral College Competition, Party Leadership, and Democratic Regulatory Choice, 1884–1936*. New York: Cambridge University Press.

Jones, Charles O. 1995. "A Way of Life and Law: Presidential Address, American Political Science Association, 1994." *American Political Science Review* 89(1): 1–9.

Jordan, Richard, Daniel Maliniak, Amy Oakes, Susan Peterson and Michael J. Tierney. 2009. "One Discipline or Many? TRIP Survey of International Relations Faculty in Ten Countries." Technical report of the Teaching, Research, and International Policy (TRIP) Project. Williamsburg, VA: Institute for the Theory and Practice of International Relations.

Katzenstein, Peter J., Robert O. Keohane, and Stephen D. Krasner. 1998. "International Organization and the Study of World Politics." *International Organization* 52(4): 645–85.

Katznelson, Ira. 1981. *City Trenches: Urban Politics and the Patterning of Class in the United States*. New York: Pantheon Books.

——. 1997. "Structure and Configuration in Comparative Politics." In *Comparative Politics: Rationality, Culture, and Structure*. New York: Cambridge University Press.

——. 2003. "Periodization and Preferences: Reflections on Purposive Action in comparative historical social science." *Comparative historical analysis in the social sciences* pp. 270–301.

Katznelson, Ira, Kim Geiger, and Daniel Kryder. 1993. "Limiting Liberalism: The Southern Veto in Congress, 1933–1950." *Political Research Quarterly* 108(2): 283–306.

Katznelson, Ira, and John S. Lapinski. 2006a. "At the Crossroads: Congress and American Political Development." *Perspectives on Politics* 4(2): 243–60.

——. 2006b. "Studying Policy Content and Legislative Behavior." In *Macropolitics of Congress*. Princeton, NJ: Princeton University Press.

Katznelson, Ira, John Lapinski, and David Bateman. 2012. "Southern Politics Revisited: On V. O. Key's 'South in the House'." Unpublished paper, University of Pennsylvania.

Kaufman, Burton I. 1993. *The Presidency of James Earl Carter Jr.* Lawrence: University Press of Kansas.

Kelly, Sean. 1993. "Divided We Govern? A Reassessment." *Polity* 25: 475–84.

Key, V. O., Jr. 1955. "A Theory of Critical Elections." *Journal of Politics* 17: 3–18.

Keyssar, Alexander. 2009. *The Right to Vote: The Contested History of Democracy in the United States*. Rev. ed. New York: Basic Books.

King, Desmond S. 1995. *Separate and Unequal: Black Americans and the U.S. Federal Government*. Oxford: Oxford University Press.

King, Desmond S., and Rogers M. Smith. 2005. "Racial Orders in American Political Development." *American Political Science Review* 99: 75–92.

Kingdon, John. 1984. *Agendas, Alternatives, and Public Policies*. Boston: Little, Brown.

Krehbiel, Keith. 1991. *Information and Legislative Organization*. Ann Arbor: University of Michigan Press.

——. 1998. *Pivotal Politics: A Theory of U.S. Lawmaking*. Chicago: University of Chicago Press.

Krehbiel, Keith, Adam Meirowitz, and Jonathan Woon. 2005. "Testing Theories of Lawmaking." In *Social Choice and Strategic Decisions: Essays in Honor of Jeffrey S. Banks*. New York: Springer.

Krutz, Glen. 2001. *Hitching a Ride: Omnibus Legislating in the U.S. Congress*. Columbus: Ohio State University Press.

Kryder, Daniel. 2000. *Divided Arsenal: Race and the American State During World War II*. New York: Cambridge University Press.

Lapinski, John S. 2000. "Representation and Reform: A Congress-Centered Approach to American Political Development." PhD thesis, Columbia University.
——. 2008. "Policy Substance and Performance in American Lawmaking, 1877–1994." *American Journal of Political Science* 52(2): 235–51.
Laski, Harold Joseph. 1917. *Studies in the Problem of Sovereignty*. New Haven, CT: Yale University Press.
Lee, Erika. 2002. "The Chinese Exclusion Example: Race, Immigration, and American Gatekeeping, 1882–1924." *Journal of American Ethnic History* 21(3): 36–62.
Leuchtenburg, William E. 1963. *Franklin D. Roosevelt and the New Deal, 1932–1940*. New York: Harper & Row.
Levinson, Sanford, and Bartholomew H. Sparrow. 2005. *The Louisiana Purchase and American Expansion, 1803–1898*. Lanham, MD: Rowman & Littlefield.
Lieberman, Robert C. 2002. "Ideas, Institutions, and Political Order: Explaining Political Change." *American Political Science Review* 96: 697–712.
Light, Paul. 2002. *Government's Greatest Achievements: From Civil Rights to Homeland Defense*. Washington, DC: Brookings Institution Press.
Link, Arthur S. 1954. *Woodrow Wilson and the Progressive Era, 1910–1917*. New York: Harper & Row.
Lowi, Theodore J. 1964. "American Business, Public Policy, Case-Studies, and Political Theory." *World Politics* 16(4): 677–715.
——. 1970. "Decision Making vs. Policy Making: Toward an Antidote for Technocracy." *Public Administration Review* 30: 314–25.
——. 1972. "Four Systems of Policy, Politics, and Choice." *Public Administration Review* 32: 298–310.
MacNeil, Neil. 1970. *Dirksen: Portrait of a Public Man*. New York: World Publishing Co.
Manin, Bernard. 1997. *The Principles of Representative Government*. New York: Cambridge University Press.
Marshall, Thomas H. 1950. *Citizenship and Social Class, and Other Essays*. Cambridge: Cambridge University Press.
Martin, Andrew D., and Kevin M. Quinn. 2002. "Dynamic Ideal Point Estimation via Markov Chain Monte Carlo for the U.S. Supreme Court, 1953–1999." *Political Analysis* 10(2): 134–53.
Mason, Edward S. and Thomas S. Lamont. 1982. "The Harvard Department of Economics from the Beginning to World War II." *Quarterly Journal of Economics* 97(3): 383–433.
——. 1986. *The Unraveling of America: A History of Liberalism in the 1960s*. New York: Harper & Row.
Mayhew, David R. 1966. *Party Loyalty Among Congressmen: The Difference Between Democrats and Republicans, 1947–1962*. Cambridge, MA: Harvard University Press.
——. 1991. *Divided We Govern: Party Control, Lawmaking, and Investigations, 1946–1990*. New Haven, CT: Yale University Press.
——. 1993. "Let's Stick with the Longer List." *Polity* 25: 485–88.
——. 2000. *America's Congress: Actions in the Public Sphere, James Madison Through Newt Gingrich*. New Haven, CT: Yale University Press.
——. 2002. *Electoral Realignments: A Critique of an American Genre*. New Haven, CT: Yale University Press.

———. 2005a. "Events as Causes: The Case of American Politics." Unpublished paper, Yale University.

———. 2005b. "Wars and American Politics." *Perspectives on Politics* 3(3): 473–93.

———. 2006. "Lawmaking and History." In *Macropolitics of Congress*. Princeton, NJ: Princeton University Press.

McCarty, Nolan, Keith Poole, and Howard Rosenthal. 2006. *Polarized America: The Dance of Ideology and Unequal Riches*. Cambridge, MA: MIT Press.

McCoy, Donald R. 1984. *The Presidency of Harry S. Truman*. Lawrence: University Press of Kansas.

McJimsey, George T. 2000. *The Presidency of Franklin Delano Roosevelt*. Lawrence: University Press of Kansas.

Mettler, Suzanne. 1998. "Dividing Social Citizenship by Gender: The Implementation of Unemployment Insurance and Aid to Dependent Children, 1935–1950." *Studies in American Political Development* 12(2): 303–42.

Mowry, George E. 1958. *The Era of Theodore Roosevelt, 1900–1912*. New York: Harper & Row.

Ngai, Mae M. 2004. *Impossible Subjects: Illegal Aliens and the Making of Modern America*. Princeton, NJ: Princeton University Press.

Nye, Joseph S., and Sean M. Lynn-Jones. 1988. "International Security Studies: A report of a Conference on the State of the Field." *International Security* 12(4): 5–27.

Orren, Karen, and Stephen Skowronek. 1994. "Beyond the iconography of order: notes for a new institutionalism." *The dynamics of American politics: Approaches and interpretations* pp. 311–30.

———. 2004. *The Search for American Political Development*. New York: Cambridge University Press.

Pach, Chester J., Jr., and Elmo Richardson. 1991. *The Presidency of Dwight D. Eisenhower*. Lawrence: University Press of Kansas.

Paul, Justus F. 1975. "Power of Seniority: Senator Hugh Butler and Statehood for Hawaii." *Hawaiian Journal of History* 9: 140–47.

Peltzman, Sam. 1984. "Constituent Interest and Congressional Voting." *Journal of Law and Economics* 27(1): 181–210.

Peterson, Eric. 2001. "Is It Science Yet? Replicating and Validating the 'Divided We Govern' List of Important Statuses." Paper presented to the annual meeting of the Midwest Political Science Association.

Pierson, Paul. 1993. "When Effect Becomes Cause: Policy Feedback and Political Change." *World Politics* 45: 595–628.

———. 1994. *Dismantling the Welfare State? Reagan, Thatcher, and the Politics of Retrenchment*. New York: Cambridge University Press.

———. 2000. "Increasing Returns, Path Dependence, and the Study of Politics." *American Political Science Review* 94(2): 251–67.

Pierson, Paul, and Theda Skocpol. 2002. "Historical Institutionalism in Contemporary Political Science." In *Political Science: State of the Discipline*. New York: W. W. Norton & Co.

Plotke, David. 1996. *Building a Democratic Political Order: Reshaping American Liberalism in the 1930s and 1940s*. New York: Cambridge University Press.

Poole, Keith T., and Howard Rosenthal. 1985. "A Spatial Model for Legislative Roll Call Analysis." *American Journal of Political Science* 29(2): 357–84.

———. 1991. "Patterns of Congressional Voting." *American Journal of Political Science* 35(1): 228–78.

———. 1997. *Congress: A Political-Economic History of Roll Call Voting.* New York: Oxford University Press.

Przeworski, Adam, Susan C. Stokes, and Bernard Manin. 1999. *Democracy, Accountability, and Representation.* New York: Cambridge University Press.

Reynolds, John. 1995. "Divided We Govern: Research Note." Unpublished paper, University of Texas at San Antonio.

Ritter, Gretchen. 1997. *Goldbugs and Greenbacks: The Antimonopoly Tradition and the Politics of Finance.* New York: Cambridge University Press.

———. 2000. "Gender and Citizenship After the Nineteenth Amendment." *Polity* 32(3): 345–76.

Rohde, David W. 1991. *Parties and Leaders in the Post-Reform House.* Chicago: University of Chicago Press.

Sanders, Elizabeth. 1999. *Roots of Reform: Farmers, Workers, and the American State.* Chicago: University of Chicago Press.

Schaller, Michael. 1992. *Reckoning with Reagan: America and Its President in the 1980s.* New York: Oxford University Press.

Schickler, Eric. 2001. *Disjointed Pluralism: Institutional Innovation and the Development of the U.S. Congress.* Princeton, NJ: Princeton University Press.

Shanks, Cheryl. 2001. *Immigration and the Politics of American Sovereignty, 1890–1990.* Ann Arbor: University of Michigan Press.

Shefter, Martin. 1977. "Party and Patronage: Germany, England, and Italy." *Politics and Society* 7: 403–51.

Sinclair, Barbara. 1978. "From Party Voting to Regional Fragmentation: The House of Representatives." *American Politics Quarterly* 6: 125–46.

Skocpol, Theda. 1992. *Protecting Soldiers and Mothers: The Political Origins of Social Policy in the United States.* Cambridge, MA: Belknap Press of Harvard University Press.

———. 1996. *Boomerang: Clinton's Health Security Effort and the Turn Against Government in U.S. Politics.* New York: W. W. Norton & Co.

Skowronek, Stephen. 1982. *Building a New American State: The Expansion of National Administrative Capacities, 1877–1920.* New York: Cambridge University Press.

———. 1997. *The Politics Presidents Make: Leadership from John Adams to Bill Clinton.* Cambridge, MA: Belknap Press of Harvard University Press.

Sloan, Irving. 1984. *American Landmark Legislation.* Dobbs Ferry, NY: Oceana Publications.

Small, Melvin. 1999. *The Presidency of Richard Nixon.* Lawrence: University Press of Kansas.

Smith, Rogers M. 1993. "Beyond Tocqueville, Myrdal, and Hartz: The Multiple Traditions in America." *American Political Science Review* 87: 549–66.

———. 1997. *Civic Ideals: Conflicting Visions of Citizenship in U.S. History.* New Haven, CT: Yale University Press.

———. 2003. *Stories of Peoplehood: The Politics and Morals of Political Membership.* New York: Cambridge University Press.

Socolofsky, Homer B., and Allan B. Spetter. 1987. *The Presidency of Benjamin Harrison*. Lawrence: University Press of Kansas.

Stathis, Stephen W. 2003. *Landmark Legislation, 1774–2002*. Washington, DC: Congressional Quarterly Press.

Stewart, Charles, and Barry R. Weingast. 1992. "Stacking the Senate, Changing the Nation: Republican Rotten Boroughs, Statehood Politics, and American Political Development." *Studies in American Political Development* 6(2): 223–71.

Strange, Susan. 1970. "International Economics and International Relations: A Case of Mutual Neglect." *International Affairs* (*Royal Institute of International Affairs 1944–*) 46(2): 304–15.

Sundquist, James L. 1988. "Needed: A Political Theory for the New Era of Coalition Government in the United States." *Political Science Quarterly* 103(4): 613–35.

Tichenor, Daniel J. 2002. *Dividing Lines: The Politics of Immigration Control in America*. Princeton, NJ: Princeton University Press.

Tilly, Charles. 1975. *The Formation of National States in Western Europe*. Princeton, NJ: Princeton University Press.

Tirole, Jean. 1988. *The Theory of Industrial Organization*. Cambridge, MA: MIT Press.

Trani, Eugene P., and David L. Wilson. 1977. *The Presidency of Warren G. Harding*. Lawrence: University Press of Kansas.

Truman, David B. 1959. *The Congressional Party: A Case Study*. New York: Wiley.

U.S. Commission on Civil Rights. 1959. *Report of the United States Commission on Civil Rights*. Technical report. Washington, DC: U.S. Commission on Civil Rights.

Valelly, Richard M. 2004. *The Two Reconstructions: The Struggle for Black Enfranchisement*. Chicago: University of Chicago Press.

Van Doren, Peter M. 1990. "Can We Learn the Causes of Congressional Decisions from Roll Call Data?" *Legislative Studies Quarterly* 15(3): 311–40.

———. 1991. *Politics, Markets, and Congressional Policy Choices*. Ann Arbor: University of Michigan Press.

Vattel, Emer de. 1916. *Le Droit des gens*. Washington, DC: Carnegie Institute of Washington.

Wawro, Gregory, and Eric Schickler. 2004. "Where's the Pivot? Obstruction and Lawmaking in the Pre-Cloture Senate." *American Journal of Political Science* 48: 758–74.

Weingast, Barry R. 1979. "A Rational Choice Perspective on Congressional Norms." *American Journal of Political Science* 24: 245–62.

Weir, Margaret. 1992. *Politics and Jobs: The Boundaries of Employment Policy in the United States*. Princeton, NJ: Princeton University Press.

Welch, Richard E., Jr. 1988. *The Presidencies of Grover Cleveland*. Lawrence: University Press of Kansas.

Westerfield, H. Bradford. 1955. *Foreign Policy and Party Politics: Pearl Harbor to Korea*. New Haven, CT: Yale University Press.

Whittington, Keith E. 1999. "What's the Point of APD?" *Clio* 5: 43–45.

Wilson, Rich K. 1986. "An Empirical Test of Preferences for the Political Pork Barrel: District-Level Appropriations for River and Harbor Legislations." *American Journal of Political Science* 30(4): 729–54.

Wirls, Daniel. 1999. "Regionalism, Rotten Boroughs, Race, and Realignment: The Seventeenth Amendment and the Politics of Representation." *Studies in American Political Development* 13(1): 1–30.

Zolberg, Aristide. 2006. *A Nation by Design: Immigration Policy in the Fashioning of the United States, 1750–2000.* Cambridge, MA, and New York: Harvard University Press and Russell Sage Foundation.

Zolberg, Aristide R. and Peter M. Benda. 2001. *Global Migrants, Global Refugees: Problems and Solutions.* New York: Berghahn Books.

Index